ALL ABOUT
BREAKFAST & BRUNCH

IRMA S. ROMBAUER
MARION ROMBAUER BECKER
ETHAN BECKER

PHOTOGRAPHY BY TUCKER & HOSSLER

SCRIBNER

NEW YORK · LONDON · TORONTO · SYDNEY · SINGAPORE

SCRIBNER
1230 Avenue of the Americas
New York, NY 10020

WELDON OWEN INC.
Chief Executive Officer: John Owen
President: Terry Newell
Chief Operating Officer: Larry Partington
Vice President, International Sales: Stuart Laurence
Publisher: Roger Shaw
Creative Director: Gaye Allen
Associate Publisher: Val Cipollone
Associate Editor: Anna Mantzaris
Consulting Editors: Judith Dunham, Norman Kolpas
Designers: Sarah Gifford, Jamie Leighton
Photo Editor: Lisa Lee
Production Director: Stephanie Sherman
Production Manager: Chris Hemesath
Production Assistant: Donita Boles
Studio Manager: Brynn Breuner
Food Stylists: Kim Konecny, Erin Quon
Cover Food Stylist: Heidi Gintner
Step-by-Step Photographer: Mike Falconer
Step-by-Step Food Stylist: Andrea Lucich

Joy of Cooking All About series was designed
and produced by Weldon Owen Inc.,
814 Montgomery Street, San Francisco,
California 94133

Set in Joanna MT and Gill Sans

Separations by Bright Arts Singapore
Printed in Singapore by Tien Wah Press (Pte.) Ltd.

10 9 8 7 6 5 4 3 2 1

Library of Congress Cataloging-in-Publication Data
is available.

ISBN 0-7432-0642-8

Recipe shown on half-title page: *Beignets, 71*
Recipe shown on title page: *Eggs in Ramekins with Ratatouille, 28*

CONTENTS

FOREWORD

Even in 1931, when my Granny Rom introduced breakfast menu-planning in the first edition of Joy of Cooking, *she noted, "To balance the New Englander's codfish balls and baked beans, the Southerner's grits and bacon, and the Northerner's fried cakes and doughnuts, there is the modern trend to make the first meal of the day as light as possible."*

While you won't find beans or codfish here, this volume in the new All About *series aims to provide a wide range of morning choices. I think you will discover that the recipes in this book reflect how little our attitudes toward breakfast and brunch have changed down through the years, whether you want a robust array of foods for a special occasion or something fresh and light to start the day.*

You might notice that this collection of kitchen-tested recipes is adapted from the latest edition of the Joy of Cooking. *Just as our family has done for generations, we have worked to make this version of* Joy *a little bit better than the last. As a result, you'll find that some notes, recipes, and techniques have been changed to improve their clarity and usefulness. Since 1931, the* Joy of Cooking *has constantly evolved. And now, the* All About *series has taken* Joy *to a whole new stage, as you will see from the beautiful color photographs of finished dishes and clearly illustrated instructions for preparing and serving them. Granny Rom and Mom would have been delighted.*

I'm sure you'll find All About Breakfast & Brunch *to be both a useful and an enduring companion in your kitchen.*

Enjoy!

Ethan Becker pictured with his grandmother, Irma von Starkloff Rombauer (left), and his mother, Marion Rombauer Becker (right). Irma Rombauer published the first Joy of Cooking at her own expense in 1931. Marion Rombauer Becker became coauthor in 1951. Joy as it has progressed through the decades (from top left to bottom right): the 1931 edition with Marion's depiction of St. Martha of Bethany, said to be the patron saint of cooking, "slaying the dragon of kitchen drudgery"; the 1943 edition; the 1951 edition; the 1962 edition; the 1975 edition; and the 1997 edition.

About Breakfast & Brunch

When you want to take the time to prepare a home-cooked meal, dinner is undoubtedly the meal you have in mind. Yet the first meal of the day—be it breakfast or brunch—can be just as rewarding to make, and it can be a satisfying and healthful way to get you ready for the tasks ahead.

At a time when so many of us seem to be working harder than ever, breakfast, especially the weekday variety, is all too often a meal of diminished importance. Even on a busy day, though, making breakfast doesn't have to be a time-consuming affair, and enjoying it need not be rushed. It really doesn't take long to brew your own cup of coffee or tea, scramble some eggs, toast bread, and cut up fresh fruit. Nor do you need much time to make a mug of hot chocolate while you reheat a muffin that you baked fresh on the weekend and stored in the freezer.

In this book, you'll find plenty of ideas that will allow you to enjoy breakfast, no matter how hectic your morning. On a weekend, you can bake not only muffins, but also delicious coffeecakes, scones, and breads, and serve them throughout the week. With a little advance planning, you can make your own cereal blends for muesli or granola and store them in a cupboard as you would purchased cereals.

Homemade fruit compotes and applesauce keep well in the refrigerator for several days. Pancake batter can largely be prepared in advance, leaving only the final mixing to be completed before the pancakes are briefly cooked. And don't forget that cobblers and crisps baked the night before make a sublime breakfast treat.

When breakfast is delayed until late morning or midday, it becomes that charming social hour called "brunch," a hybrid of breakfast and lunch first used in England in the late nineteenth century and popularized in the United States in the 1930s. Brunch can also be an easy meal to prepare and may be served buffet style (opposite) or may more closely resemble a light lunch.

Choose your brunch menu carefully, keeping it simple. If you don't have time to do your own baking, offering bakery scones, muffins, bagels, and fancy breads is perfectly acceptable—and a good way for beginners to practice their entertaining skills. At first, you may want to avoid complicated egg dishes that might be difficult to prepare for a crowd—individual omelets or eggs Benedict, for example. Quiche Lorraine, frittatas, and tortilla Española are popular egg-based brunch specialties, because they can be made ahead. Along with coffee and tea, it is customary to serve something alcoholic with brunch, such as white wine, Champagne (or the combination of Champagne and orange juice known as the Mimosa), or a pitcher of Bloody Marys. As you gain confidence in your entertaining skills, you can prepare more elaborate menus for a larger number of guests.

Morning Entertaining

One of the most leisurely ways to entertain is to have people over for brunch late on a weekend morning. People are relaxed, conversation flows easily, and guests linger happily at table. The menu is often easier to prepare and serve than menus offered at other times of day, making the occasion as pleasurable for hosts as it is for guests.

As at dinner, we find that the most easily managed and congenial number of guests for a morning meal is between six and eight—enough to encourage social interaction in numerous configurations but not so many that conversation turns to a din. Some occasions may call for many more guests, in which case you should follow our suggestions

for hosting a brunch buffet (below). Invite friends you think will genuinely enjoy one another, whether or not they've ever met. Invitations, whether by phone or in writing, should go out two to three weeks in advance; for a party on or near a major holiday, contact guests at least a month ahead of time, as schedules can be busy.

RULES FOR BRUNCH BUFFETS

- Buffets are a good choice for large, casual brunch get-togethers when dining-table space is limited.

- Choose a colorful, varied array of foods and display them on a handsomely appointed table.

- Make sure you have ample backup portions of everything served, so you can replenish dishes as needed. Cater generously, for guests are apt to take larger portions at buffets.

- Label any food that isn't easily identifiable with a small card placed beside the dish.

- If you're having more than a dozen guests, set up two identical buffet lines so guests can serve themselves quickly and still have a chance to sample everything. Make sure that there is an ample supply of plates and utensils for both lines.

- If you are low on casseroles or hot plates, restrict the number of hot foods to those you can serve quickly straight from the pot or a hot serving dish, or obtain more serving vessels from a party rental company.

- Everything offered on a buffet should be easily eaten with a fork or with fingers—no knife cutting required.

Table Settings

An inviting table is as important as inviting food. Table decorations can be as natural or whimsical as you like, but make sure they don't interfere with the passing of serving dishes or block guests' views of one another—and remember that they should be suited in color and scale to the foods served. Don't make the effects so stagy that your guests' reaction is "You went to a lot of trouble." Make them say, rather, "You had a lot of fun doing it!"

Flowers should have no detectable scent; heavy perfumes of any kind fight with the flavors of the food. Arrange flowers in small bouquets or consider floating rosebuds or other flowers in shallow bowls or custard cups. (It's a good idea

to have an empty vase or two on hand in case guests bring flowers with them. Such flowers needn't go on the dining table but can be placed on a sideboard or in the living room.)

Napkins should be simply folded into quarters and then in half into rectangles or triangles. The exposed corner faces the bottom left, making it easy for the seated guests to pick up the napkin by one corner, let it drop and unfold completely, and place it on his or her lap.

Most brunches will call for just a single dinner plate to be placed at each place; for some foods, these may be heated in the kitchen (opposite) and brought to the table with food on them after guests are seated.

Salad plates may be used for the fruit courses that are often served with brunch. If you like, add small butter plates just to the left of each setting for toast, muffins, or other morning breads. Set out good-sized juice glasses, too, before the meal, positioned just above and to the right of each setting.

Practicality guides both host and guest in the setting and use of silverware. The simple rule is to work from the outside in, with as many forks as are needed placed to the left of the main-course plate and the knife to the right. If you're setting a butter plate and have butter knives, these should be placed on each butter plate in a position mimicking that of the main-course knife.

Planning Breakfast and Brunch Menus

When we think of combining dishes to make a menu, we like to recall the aphorism of the great French gastronome Brillat-Savarin: *Menu malfait, diner perdu*—"A badly made menu means a lost dinner." In planning breakfasts or brunches, simple or elaborate, first consider the season, the climate, and the probable likes and dislikes of those at table. When entertaining people whose tastes one does not know, it is a good idea to consider familiar foods that almost everyone loves.

Following are some suggested menus for breakfasts and brunches. Your tastes, circumstances, market, mood—and, we hope, imagination—will modify them considerably. Add your and your guests' choice of coffee, tea, hot chocolate, or milk.

CLASSIC AMERICAN
Fresh Fruit Cup, 83
French Scrambled Eggs, 25
Sautéed Bacon, 40
Buttermilk Biscuits, 108, and honey

FRENCH FAVORITES
Orange and Tomato Juice, 18
Savory Cheese and Herb-Filled
    Souffléed Omelet, 32
Pommes Anna, 45

FESTIVE FARE
Bellini, 20
Onion Frittata with Sherry Vinegar
    Sauce, 33
Four-Strand Braided Challah, 118

BRUNCH ENTERTAINING
Bloody Mary, 21
Crabcakes, 42
Basted Fried Eggs, 24
Deluxe Sunday Morning
    Coffeecake, 110

COUNTRY STYLE
Cornmeal Waffles, 63
Chicken and Apple Sausage, 38
Old-Fashioned Lemonade, 18

FRUITY BREAKFAST
Three-Grain Apple Cinnamon
    Granola, 75
Half-Covered Berry or Peach
    Galette, 100

HEATING PLATES

Some hot breakfast and brunch dishes such as eggs, pancakes, and waffles benefit from being served on heated plates. When you plan to heat plates, use your everyday china, which might better withstand heating, checking manufacturer's information (or, sometimes, the undersides of the plates) for any precautions. If you've deemed the plates heatproof, place them on the rack in a 175°F oven for about 15 minutes, then remove them with a potholder. The drying cycle of a dishwasher will also heat plates, or you can simply run them under hot tap water and dry them just before serving.

ABOUT
BEVERAGES

*M*ore than at any other time of day, we look to breakfast and brunch to revive and refresh ourselves. That explains why so many of us regard beverages as one of the most important considerations—when we're pressed for time, the only consideration—at a morning meal.

Coffee and tea are often in the spotlight because of the power their caffeine content has to help increase alertness. We are happy to see, however, how much attention has been paid in recent years to brewing both these morning drinks properly, using the finest coffee beans or tea leaves available and preparing them fresh, with an awareness of the finer points of preparation that bring out their best. Even if you prefer decaffeinated coffee or herbal tea, such attention to detail brings enormous benefits to your morning cup. It also does the same for even a simple glass of juice.

Sometimes, of course, beverages have the opposite goal of the everyday hot brews. Drinks like the Mimosa, 20, or the Bloody Mary, 21, aim to promote relaxation at a weekend brunch. Served responsibly and enjoyed in moderation, they can bring a most pleasurable aspect to morning entertaining.

Clockwise from left: *Cappuccino, 14; Caffè Latte, 14; Espresso, 14*

Grinding Coffee Beans and Brewing Coffee

It is essential to use the right grind of coffee for your brewing method. As a rule of thumb, the shorter the brewing time, the finer the grind must be. Espresso, which brews in 30 seconds or less, requires a very fine grind. Plunger-pot coffee, in which coffee grounds steep in water for a full 6 minutes, requires a very coarse grind. Propeller-blade grinders, the kind most people have, are not ideal, for they produce an uneven grind and can heat the beans, thereby releasing aromatic substances that should go into your cup and not into the air. Cool, precise tearing apart of the beans is best done in a burr mill, which has two notched blades whose position can be set for the desired fineness of grinds. Follow the manufacturer's instructions for grinding times. If you don't own a burr mill, you can use one of the professional ones commonly found at supermarkets.

If you must use a propeller-blade grinder, grind the beans slightly coarser than you think you'll need, grind in 10-second bursts, and never whir the beans for more than 30 seconds, which will overheat them. Try not to grind more than ½ cup beans at a time. Lift the machine off the counter and shake it while it grinds. The grounds should resemble coarse-ground cornmeal for a plunger pot and granulated sugar for a drip brewer.

The ratio of ground coffee to water is vital: The general rule is to use 1 standard coffee scoop, which holds 2 tablespoons ground coffee, for every 6 ounces water. The problem is that coffee scoops tend to vary greatly in capacity. Measure the capacity of your scoop and adjust your subsequent coffee measurements accordingly. If you prefer weaker coffee, make it at full strength and then dilute it to taste with hot water or milk.

There are a number of good ways to brew coffee, but the percolator is not one of them. Percolators violate two of the cardinal rules of good coffee brewing: they boil the coffee, encouraging bitter and sour flavors, and they pour water that is too hot over the grounds repeatedly, instead of just-right water only once.

ESPRESSO, CAPPUCCINO, AND CAFFÈ LATTE

The term *espresso* correctly refers to the brewing method, not a coffee bean or degree of roast, and it's the brewing method that gives the fullest-bodied coffee by far. Espresso machines force hot but not boiling water through finely ground coffee at high pressure. The pressure produces a syrupy body impossible to achieve by any other means and a pleasantly bittersweet flavor that lingers on the palate. The trade-off for the matchless concentration of flavor that espresso provides is that you get only a very small amount at a time. A properly brewed cup of espresso measures just 1½ to 2 ounces, as compared with the 6 ounces in a standard cup of coffee as calculated by the coffee industry. You need special equipment to make espresso—either a moka pot for stovetop brewing or an electric pump espresso maker. Both are commonly available.

Cappuccino—named for the brown robes of Capuchin monks, whose color it is thought to resemble—is the glory of the Italian coffee bar. True cappuccino is just espresso and steamed milk crowned by a head of satiny foam—with coffee, milk, and foam in approximately equal proportions. (Steamed milk is simply milk that has been heated with an injection of steam, usually through a tube connected to the boiler of an espresso machine.) To make cappuccino, first steam the milk (follow the manufacturer's instructions on your espresso machine or simply scald the milk in a saucepan, making certain that it does not come to a boil), aiming for a combination of milk and foam that is about twice the volume of the milk you started with. Then brew espresso into a larger cup than usual. Using a large spoon to block the foam so that hot milk comes out of the pitcher first, pour no more than ½ cup milk over the waiting espresso—¼ cup steamed milk and ¼ cup foam is ideal. Spread the foam gently over the top of the espresso, leaving visible a brown rim around the edge.

Caffè latte is basically an oversized cappuccino in the United States, but in Italy it is one part espresso diluted with four parts scalded or steamed milk, with no foam on top. Caffè macchiato is espresso "marked" with just a tablespoon or two of foam. In Italy, coffee with milk is considered a breakfast beverage; after lunch or dinner, Italians drink espresso.

Cocoa and Hot Chocolate

Cocoa powder, from which most hot chocolate (more correctly, hot cocoa) is made, is often sold pre-mixed with powdered milk and sugar. Because cocoa powder does not dissolve instantly in liquid but tends to form lumps that must be smoothed by vigorous stirring, commercial mixes are treated to increase solubility. You will have much better hot chocolate if you start with unsweetened cocoa powder, sweeten it to taste, and mix it with fresh milk. Some cocoa powder has been "Dutched" by the addition of an alkaline agent. Dutch processing darkens cocoa powder to a lustrous mahogany color and helps make it more soluble, but does not necessarily improve the flavor. To fluff chocolate drinks just before serving and to inhibit the formation of the cream "skin" on top, try mixing with a wire whisk or rotary beater. Serve the hot beverage in a deep, narrow cup to retain the heat, and spoon whipped cream on top if desired.

American Hot Cocoa

1 cup

This is easily doubled.
Stir together in a small, heavy saucepan:
1 tablespoon unsweetened cocoa
1 teaspoon sugar
Vigorously stir in, first by table-spoons and then in a slow, steady stream:
¾ cup milk
Heat, stirring constantly and scraping the bottom of the pan, over medium heat just until bubbles appear at the sides. Remove from the heat and stir in:
⅛ teaspoon vanilla
Top with:
Ground nutmeg or cinnamon
Whipped cream or marshmallows

Italian Hot Cocoa

2½ cups

Stir together in a medium, heavy saucepan:
½ cup unsweetened cocoa
⅓ cup sugar
1 teaspoon cornstarch or
    arrowroot
Stir in thoroughly and set over low heat:
½ cup water
Stir in:
½ cup water
1 cup milk
Cook, stirring, over medium-low heat until the mixture is thickened and coats a spoon, about 10 minutes. Stir in:
⅛ teaspoon vanilla (optional)
Top each serving with:
Ground nutmeg or cinnamon
Whipped cream or marshmallows

French Hot Chocolate

6 cups

A richer, sweeter beverage than cocoa.
In a medium, heavy saucepan, bring to a rolling boil:
1 cup light or heavy cream
Immediately remove from the heat and whisk in:
8 ounces bittersweet or semisweet
    chocolate, cut into ¼-inch pieces
Strain the mixture through a fine-mesh sieve, pushing it through with a rubber spatula. Refrigerate the chocolate concentrate in a covered jar for up to 10 days.
For each cup of hot chocolate, stir together:
¼ cup chocolate concentrate
¼ cup milk, water, or coffee
Heat over low heat, or in a microwave on high for 45 to 60 seconds, until warm but not boiling. Stir in:
⅛ teaspoon vanilla (optional)
Top each serving with:
Ground nutmeg or cinnamon

Brewing Tea

All you need to brew tea well is hot water and the best tea you can find—and the water is almost as important as the tea. If the water that goes into your tea doesn't taste good, neither will the finished product. Don't use distilled water, for the minerals, essential for flavor, have been removed. Filtered water, on the other hand, is ideal.

Your teapot should have a wide mouth, for getting tea in and out of the pot, and a handle that stays cool. Avoid aluminum and uncoated metal, which will interact with the tea and produce off flavors. Our favorite pot contains a wide and deep inset wire mesh basket, which gives plenty of room for the tea leaves to expand and can be lifted out as soon as the tea is ready. The mesh allows easier contact between water and tea than glazed ceramic baskets, whose perforations tend to be stingy. Individual metal tea filters

are also available and useful. Look for the ones that offer the most water-tea contact.

The traditional measure for tea is one teaspoon tea per cup and one for the pot, but in fact, the amount of tea should vary according to your own taste and the kind of tea you're using. The less the tea has been processed, the more you'll need. As a starting point, use the above measure for black tea, half again as much for oolong, and twice as much for green tea. Length of brewing time also should vary according to tea type—as well as whether the tea is loose or in bags. (Tea bags steep the fastest.) *Tea is not ready when its color changes.* This is one of the most common mistakes people make in brewing tea. Tea bags should steep for at least three minutes and no more than five; oolongs, Darjeelings, and delicate black teas usually require three to four minutes; other

black teas need four to five minutes; green teas should steep for only one to two minutes. Tea should never steep in hot water for longer than five minutes or it will be bitter.

Always preheat the teapot. Water for brewing most teas must be boiling hot; the exception is green tea, for which the water should be hot but not boiling (170° to 190°F). Always bring the teapot to the kettle, not vice versa, so the water will not have time to cool. To keep tea warm both during and after brewing, you may wrap the teapot in a tea cozy or thick towel. Once you've removed the leaves, tea may be transferred to a thermal carafe. (Don't use a carafe you've put coffee in, however, or your tea will take on a coffee flavor). To serve tea to a crowd, brew in advance a pot using twice as much tea as usual, then fill each cup or pot with half tea essence and half hot water as needed.

HERBAL TEAS

These are not really teas but rather infusions (the French call them *tisanes*) made not with tea leaves but with herbs. Both soothing and refreshing, herbal teas traditionally have been used medicinally. Among the most popular herbal teas are chamomile (a reputed stomach settler), peppermint, rose hips, *tilleul* (the French word for leaves of the European linden, or lime, tree), and lemon verbena (*verveine*). These are brewed alone or in blends. Feel free to create your own blends, including whatever spices you like or bits of fresh lemon grass and ginger.

Spiced Tea

8 servings

Combine in a saucepan and bring to a boil:

½ cup sugar
¾ cup water

Remove from the heat and add:

4 strips orange zest
6 whole cloves
4 cardamom seeds, crushed
One 3-inch cinnamon stick

Meanwhile, prepare the tea (see *Brewing Tea, opposite*), using:

3 tablespoons plus 1 teaspoon loose black tea
5 cups water

Pour the hot infusion into a heavy heatproof bowl. Strain the steeped tea over the mixture and serve at once in punch cups or teacups.

Lemon Verbena (Verveine)

3 to 5 servings

This infusion method can be used for all herbal teas. The green leaves of lemon verbena have a sweet citrus fragrance.

Bring to a boil:

3 cups water

Remove from the heat and immediately pour over:

½ cup dried lemon verbena (verveine) leaves

set in a strainer insert (see *Brewing Tea, opposite*) or in a teapot. Let steep for 10 to 20 minutes. Remove the insert or strain out the leaves and serve at once in teacups.

Iced Tea

8 servings

Rombauer family legend has it that this beverage originated at the St. Louis World's Fair; the circumstance, the indifference of the general public in the sweltering midwestern heat to Richard Blechynden's hot tea concession.

Prepare the tea (see *Brewing Tea, opposite*), using twice the quantity of leaves suggested. Stir, strain, and let cool to room temperature. Pour over ice cubes in tall glasses.

Serve with your choice of:

Lemon slices
Mint sprigs or bruised mint leaves
Sugar or honey
1 teaspoon rum per serving

WHAT TO PUT IN TEA

"Milk or lemon?" "Neither, thank you," purists will reply. But milk goes well with black tea, for its sweetness counteracts the astringency of the tannins. The old-fashioned English dictate "milk in first," or "MIF"— supposedly a sign of good breeding—was simply a way to prevent thin porcelain in typically cold English houses from cracking at the touch of hot tea. Sugar also makes black tea palatable.

Old-Fashioned Lemonade

4 servings

Chilled tea may be added to either lemonade or limeade—about ⅓ cup for every cup of juice—for an invigorating lift. Add more or less sugar depending on the tartness of the lemon juice and your tastes.

Boil for 2 minutes:

4 cups water

¾ cup sugar

Refrigerate until cold, then stir in:

Juice of 2 to 3 medium lemons

Pour over ice cubes in tall glasses or into a pitcher full of ice (opposite).

Orange and Tomato Juice

4 servings

Other good juice combinations include orange and pineapple, white grape and orange, and cranberry and sweetened grapefruit.

Combine in a pitcher:

1½ cups tomato juice

1 cup orange juice (preferably freshly squeezed)

1 teaspoon sugar

1 tablespoon fresh lemon or lime juice

½ teaspoon salt

½ cup crushed ice

Fresh Pineapple Juice

3 or 4 servings

Many other varieties of fresh fruit can be turned into juice by processing in a blender or juicer. Whatever pulp remains can be removed with a slotted spoon before the juice is strained. If the juice seems too thick, dilute it with a little cold water.

Peel, core, and cut into cubes:

2 large ripe pineapples

Process in a blender or juicer, then strain the juice.

Serve it over ice with:

Mint sprigs

OLD-FASHIONED LIMEADE

In summer, when limes are less expensive than lemons—a bargain, in fact—we find new ways to use them in place of lemons in recipes such as this refreshing beverage.

Prepare the recipe for *Old-Fashioned Lemonade*, above, substituting the juice of 4 limes for that of the lemons.

JUICING CITRUS FRUITS

Pierce the fruit with a knife and microwave for 30 seconds or place in hot water for a few minutes. Then roll under your palm on a hard surface until the inside feels soft. Both heat and pressure release juice from the cells. To quickly juice a small fruit or two, cut in half, hold the cut side of a half against the palm of your hand, and squeeze firmly. Seeds will be trapped inside. To juice several fruits, use a citrus press, which often has a built-in strainer, or a wooden reamer, which requires straining the seeds from the juice. Store citrus juice in a dark glass jar with a screw lid and keep it cold. Freshly squeezed juice retains nearly all its vitamin C for about 24 hours, although its flavor will deteriorate.

Bellini

1 serving

This luxurious cocktail was invented at Harry's Bar in Venice. For an alcohol-free Baby Bellini, replace the wine with ginger ale.

In a blender, process until smooth:

½ ripe peach, peeled and pitted

Pour into a champagne flute, then fill with:

Chilled prosecco (Italian sparkling wine), Champagne, or California sparkling wine

Mimosa

1 serving

If you use freshly squeezed orange juice and a modest vintage French Champagne—or a good French, Californian, Italian, or Spanish sparkling wine—this brunch cocktail approaches true elegance.

Pour into a chilled 8-ounce champagne flute or wine glass:

¼ cup (2 ounces) orange juice (preferably freshly squeezed)

Fill the glass with:

Chilled nonvintage French Champagne or other good-quality sparkling wine

Stir once.

Kir

1 serving

Canon Félix Kir was the mayor of Dijon, France, and a hero of the Resistance during World War II. His favorite drink was then called vin blanc cassis, *based on the good white wine of the region and another local product—black currant liqueur. Locals renamed the beverage in his honor. A Kir Royale replaces the white wine with Champagne; a Kir Cardinale uses red wine in place of white.*

Combine in a large wine glass:

¾ cup (6 ounces) chilled Mâcon Blanc or other dry white wine

Dash of crème de cassis

Champagne Punch

20 servings

For a nonalcoholic Mock Champagne Punch, replace the brandy, rum, curaçao, and maraschino with a 750-ml bottle of cola and substitute soda water or a citrus-flavored soft drink for the Champagne.

Peel, core, slice, crush, and place in a large bowl:

3 ripe pineapples

Cover the pineapple and juice with:

1 pound powdered sugar

Let stand, covered, for 1 hour. Stir in:

½ bottle (about 1½ cups or 12 ounces) brandy

½ bottle (about 1½ cups or 12 ounces) light rum

2 jiggers (3 ounces) curaçao

2 jiggers (3 ounces) maraschino

Juice of 12 lemons

Let stand for 4 hours. Transfer to a punch bowl with:

1 block ice

Stir to blend and chill. Just before serving, pour in:

4 bottles (750 ml each) chilled Champagne

Cooked Eggnog

About 18 servings

Lightly cooking this eggnog kills any possibly dangerous bacteria in the eggs. For an alcohol-free eggnog, 2 table-spoons of vanilla can replace the spirits. Do not double this recipe.

Combine and set aside:

1 cup milk

1 cup heavy cream

Whisk just until blended:

12 large egg yolks

1⅓ cups sugar

1 teaspoon freshly grated or ground nutmeg

Whisk in:

2 cups milk

2 cups heavy cream

Transfer the mixture to a large, heavy saucepan and place over low heat, stirring constantly, until the mixture becomes a little thicker than heavy cream (about 175°F). Do not overheat, or the mixture will curdle.

Remove from the heat and immediately stir in the reserved milk and cream. Pour through a strainer into a storage container. Chill thoroughly, uncovered, then stir in:

1½ cups brandy, Cognac, dark rum, or bourbon

Cover and refrigerate for at least 3 hours or up to 3 days. Serve sprinkled with:

Freshly grated or ground nutmeg

Bloody Mary

1 serving

This cocktail is slightly less aggressive than most. For this reason it is often served at brunch. When tequila takes the place of vodka in a Bloody Mary, it becomes a Bloody María; made with gin, it is a Ruddy Mary. Replace half the tomato juice with chilled beef bouillon or consommé and you'll have a Bloody Bull; replace it all with beef bouillon and omit the celery salt and pepper, and the result is a Bullshot. A Bloody Mary without any alcohol is a Virgin Mary.

Shake well with ice:

1 jigger (1½ ounces) vodka

4 jiggers (¾ cup or 6 ounces) tomato juice (preferably fresh)

2 or 3 drops lemon juice

2 or 3 drops Worcestershire sauce

Drop of hot red pepper sauce

Pinch of celery salt

Pinch of salt

Pinch of ground black pepper

Strain over ice in a highball glass.

Garnish with:

1 small celery stalk

ABOUT
EGGS

The egg is nature's perfect shape. It is not surprising that so elegant a container should turn out to hold a small treasure of balanced nutrients—proteins, fats, vitamins, and minerals.

Though they are most commonly thought of as morning menu items, eggs and egg dishes may be acceptably served at any meal: fried, scrambled, boiled, poached, baked, or incorporated into omelets or a soufflé. And almost unlimited variations of meat, vegetables, or fish may accompany or be folded into them.

No egg dish really succeeds, however, unless the eggs are strictly fresh and are cooked with due respect for their delicacy and sensitive response to heat. In only one type of preparation should the heat be high and brief—for omelets, 30–31. Otherwise, dishes in which eggs predominate invariably do best if gently cooked and carefully timed.

Leek Tart, 35

Making Fried Eggs

Fried eggs are actually sautéed eggs—cooked in a small amount of fat, usually butter, but sometimes bacon fat or olive or other vegetable oil. Fried eggs, like eggs cooked other ways, will quickly turn tough and rubbery if the heat is too high. There are some cooks who like the brown, crispy edges of a fast-cooked fried egg, but a lower temperature yields a tender, more delicate egg.

If you are concerned about presentation, truly fresh grade AA eggs make the best-looking fried eggs, with their neat, compact shape and high, well-centered yolk. Using a nonstick skillet makes it easier to slide the cooked eggs onto a plate. If you do not have a nonstick skillet, be sure to use enough butter or other fat to generously coat the bottom of the pan.

BASTED FRIED EGGS

For sunny-side-up eggs that are more cooked on top, cook the eggs in 2 to 3 tablespoons fat. Collect the hot fat from the edges of the pan and dribble it over the eggs. Baste in this manner 2 or 3 times, covering the pan between bastings.

Eggs Beatrice

4 servings

Heat in a large skillet over medium heat:

2 tablespoons butter

Add and cook until heated through:

4 large tomato slices, ¼ to ½ inch thick

Remove from the skillet and place 1 slice on each of:

4 English muffin halves, toasted, or 4 *Golden Potato Pancakes*, 45, each about 3 inches in diameter

Quickly wipe out the pan with a paper towel. Add:

1 tablespoon butter

When the butter is foaming, break into the skillet:

4 eggs

Season with:

Scant ⅛ teaspoon salt
Pinch of ground black pepper

Cover and cook until the whites are completely set and the yolks are just barely beginning to thicken around the edges, 4 to 6 minutes. Place the eggs on top of the tomatoes. Increase the heat to high and add to the skillet:

2 tablespoons butter
1 tablespoon minced shallots or scallions
3 tablespoons red wine vinegar

Boil the mixture until slightly reduced. Stir in:

2 tablespoons chopped mixed fresh herbs, such as parsley, tarragon, and chives

Taste and adjust the seasonings. Pour the sauce over the eggs and serve.

Egg in a Hole

1 or 2 servings

Young eaters get a kick out of this dish. Using a 2½-inch biscuit cutter or small glass, cut a round hole out of the center of:

2 slices sandwich bread

Melt in a large skillet over medium heat:

2 tablespoons butter

Add the bread slices and cook for about 30 seconds. Crack into the holes:

2 eggs

Do not worry if some of the white remains on top of the bread. Add more butter if needed. When the egg begins to set, 2 to 3 minutes, flip the bread and egg using a spatula. Fry the other side until the eggs are done to your liking. Serve on a warmed plate. Fry the leftover rounds of bread and serve them as well.

EGG SIZES

Although the most common egg size sold today is large, any size may be used for preparations such as fried, boiled, or poached—that is, when the size of the egg has no effect on the overall recipe. Otherwise, our recipes state when large eggs should be used. The typical serving is 1 or 2 eggs per person.

French Scrambled Eggs

2 servings

It takes both patience and a bit of technique to make great looking and tasting scrambled eggs. First, beat the eggs until the whites and yolks are completely blended. The addition of cream, butter, milk, or even water will keep the eggs more tender when cooked to medium doneness. But the liquid can also separate out and turn the eggs watery, especially if they are cooked too quickly—gentle heat is essential for producing soft, delectable eggs. The lower the heat, the longer it takes the eggs to cook, and the creamier the result. The French technique takes this principle to an extreme by cooking scrambled eggs in a double boiler. Infrequent stirring will produce large, uneven curds; more constant, careful stirring and scraping of the bottom of the pan will result in more delicate, billowy curds and creamier eggs. Vigorous stirring will produce small curds. Finally, scrambled eggs must be served immediately. We recommend transferring them to warmed plates while they are still slightly underdone. They will continue to cook and firm up on their way to the table.

Melt in the top of a double boiler over—not in—boiling water:

1 tablespoon butter

Beat together until the whites and yolks are completely combined:

3 to 4 eggs

2 tablespoons butter, cut into small pieces

¼ teaspoon salt

⅛ teaspoon ground black pepper

Pour the eggs into the double boiler and stir with a wooden spoon as the butter melts. Continue stirring, scraping the bottom and sides of the pan, until the eggs have thickened into soft, creamy curds, 10 to 15 minutes. Serve immediately.

Matzo Brei

1 serving

For centuries when Passover came, Jewish cooks around the world invented different ways to use matzo, unleavened bread. This recipe for matzo and eggs can compete with any brunch pancakes or waffles.

For each person use:

2 unsalted matzos

1 large egg, well beaten

Hold the matzos under hot running water to quickly wet both sides without making them soggy. Place in a colander to drain. Tear the matzos into 2½- to 3-inch pieces and set in a bowl. Add the egg and gently stir to coat the matzo pieces.

Season to taste with:

Salt

Heat in a large skillet:

⅛ inch vegetable oil or chicken fat

Spread the matzo mixture in the skillet in a very thin layer, spreading it with a large spoon or spatula. Cook, turning the pieces as they brown, until medium-brown and crispy. If making a large quantity for a crowd, use 2 pans and keep the cooked matzo brei warm in a 200°F oven. Serve warm, passing the salt shaker or a combination of sugar and cinnamon.

Eggs Benedict

2 to 4 servings

This enduring brunch specialty (opposite) was apparently invented at the famed Delmonico's restaurant in New York City in the 1920s. Then, as now, hollandaise sauce was considered essential. The basic construction lends itself to improvisation. In place of ham or Canadian bacon, the eggs can be placed on top of smoked salmon, fried tomatoes, or artichoke bottoms and set upon a base of thick-cut toast, corn bread, or potato pancakes. The eggs can even be fried or medium-boiled and carefully peeled instead of poached.

Place on warmed plates or a warmed serving platter:

2 English muffins, split, toasted, and buttered

Arrange on the muffins:

4 thick slices ham or Canadian bacon, warmed

Set on each slice of ham one of:

4 *Poached Eggs*, right, well drained

Divide among the 4 eggs to coat:

½ cup *Blender Hollandaise Sauce*, opposite

Serve immediately, passing extra sauce on the side if desired.

Eggs with Smoked Salmon

4 servings

Place on warmed plates or a warmed serving platter:

4 slices light rye or pumpernickel bread, toasted and buttered

Arrange on the toast:

4 thin slices smoked salmon

Set on each slice of salmon one of:

4 *Poached Eggs*, right, well drained

Divide among the 4 eggs to coat:

½ cup *Scandinavian Mustard-Dill Sauce*, below, or *Blender Hollandaise Sauce*, opposite

Sprinkle with:

Snipped fresh dill

Serve immediately, passing extra sauce on the side if desired.

Scandinavian Mustard-Dill Sauce

About 1 cup

Whisk together in a medium bowl until smooth:

3 tablespoons Swedish or Dijon mustard

2 tablespoons snipped fresh dill

1 to 2 tablespoons sugar

2 tablespoons fresh lemon juice or red wine vinegar, or to taste

Salt and ground black pepper to taste

Pinch of ground cardamom

Gradually add, whisking constantly, until blended and smooth:

½ cup vegetable oil

Cover and let stand for 2 to 3 hours before serving to allow the flavors to develop. Serve at room temperature or chilled. This sauce will keep, covered and refrigerated, for up to 2 days.

Poached Eggs

4 servings

Poached eggs should be poached, not simmered or boiled. Start with fresh grade AA eggs cracked just moments before cooking. While water is certainly the most common medium for poaching eggs, other liquids, including stock, wine, cream, milk, or sauce, can be used. The eggs can be poached ahead of time and refrigerated for up to 24 hours; transfer to a bowl of ice water the moment they are done, then, when ready to serve, carefully transfer to a large bowl full of 150°F water, cover, and let stand for 15 minutes.

Heat 2 to 3 inches of water in a large saucepan over medium heat until almost boiling. Add:

1 tablespoon vinegar (any type)

Crack into 4 small cups and slide one by one from the cup into the simmering water:

4 eggs

If an egg sinks to the bottom, wait until it is nearly set before attempting to dislodge it with a slotted spoon so the yolk does not break. Maintain the water just below a simmer, reducing the heat to low if necessary. Cook until the whites are set and the centers are still soft. Remove with a large slotted spoon and set in a second pan of water warmed to 150°F. Cover and let stand for 15 minutes; reheat if the temperature falls below 145°F. Drain each egg with a slotted spoon and hold it against a clean, dry dish towel to absorb as much water as possible. If desired, use scissors to trim away any ragged edges.

CLARIFIED BUTTER

Butterfat that has been separated from its water and milk keeps about three times longer, does not burn in sautéing, and has a pure clean flavor. Cut unsalted butter into small pieces and melt over low heat without stirring and without allowing the butter to sizzle, then simmer for 10 to 15 minutes. Strain the mixture well and let the clear yellow liquid cool before covering. When chilled, clarified butter becomes grainy. It should be used only in cooking.

Blender Hollandaise Sauce

About 1 cup

The clarified butter should be very warm, since the sauce is not reheated.
Place in a blender or food processor:

3 large egg yolks

2 teaspoons fresh lemon juice, or to taste

Ground white pepper or hot red pepper sauce to taste

Salt to taste

Process on high speed for 1 minute. With the machine running, add in a slow, steady stream:

½ cup very warm to hot *Clarified Butter*, left

By the time all the butter is poured in—about 1 minute—the sauce should be thickened. If not, process on high speed for about 20 seconds more. Taste and adjust the seasonings. Serve immediately or keep warm by submerging the blender container in warm (not hot) water. Serve warm.

Making Baked Eggs

There are several advantages to baking eggs. First, the heat of the oven cooks eggs slowly and evenly, eliminating many of the challenges of stovetop cooking. Next, it is both convenient and attractive to serve eggs in the little ramekins, gratin dishes, or casseroles in which they were baked (the French call this presentation *en cocotte*). Finally, this method is wonderfully flexible. Classically speaking, baked, or shirred, eggs are cooked in buttered molds with nothing more than salt and pepper and a little butter or cream. Sautéed vegetables, cooked breakfast meats, or smoked fish can be added to the molds, or the eggs can be topped with cheese or sauces of various kinds. (If you wish to cut back on fat, eliminate the butter or cream and simply cover each dish to trap the steam and prevent the surface from drying out.)

Four-ounce ramekins, which hold one egg, are commonly used, but you can use something larger— 6-ounce custard cups, ovenproof coffee cups, dessert bowls, or large muffin tins. Baked eggs should be cooked until the whites are set and the yolks just beginning to set. Care should be taken not to overcook the eggs: the ramekins will retain heat and continue to cook the eggs after they are removed from the oven.

Baked Eggs

1 serving

To bake 2 eggs, use a 6-ounce ramekin, double all other ingredients, and bake for about 18 minutes.

Preheat the oven to 350°F. Lightly butter a 4-ounce ramekin and sprinkle it with:

Pinch of salt
Pinch of ground black pepper

Crack into it:

1 egg

Drizzle over the top:

1 teaspoon to 1 tablespoon heavy cream
½ teaspoon melted butter (optional)

If you do not use cream or butter, loosely cover the top of the ramekin with foil. Bake in a water bath until the white is firm and the yolk is thickened, about 15 minutes. Serve directly from the ramekin with buttered toast.

> **MAKING A WATER BATH**
>
> Choose a roasting pan large enough to accommodate the molds without them touching one another, and line it with a dish towel. Slide the ramekin-filled pan into the preheated oven, and immediately pour in enough hot water to come one-half to two-thirds up the sides of the ramekins.

Eggs in Ramekins with Ratatouille

6 servings

Have ready:

1½ cups *Ratatouille*, 49

Preheat the oven to 400°F.

Lightly grease 12 ramekins, about 1½ inches deep and 3 inches in diameter with:

3 tablespoons butter

Sprinkle the bottoms with:

Salt and ground black pepper

Spoon an equal portion of the ratatouille into each ramekin, reserving a small portion for use as garnish. Cover to keep warm. Using a total of:

12 eggs

break 1 egg into each ramekin and sprinkle lightly with:

Salt and ground black pepper

Arrange the ramekins in a baking dish and pour boiling water around them. Bake until the whites are firm and the yolks are liquidy or just starting to firm, 10 to 12 minutes. Spoon a little of the reserved ratatouille on top of each serving (opposite). Serve 2 to each guest along with:

French bread or buttered toast

Cover a small plate with a napkin, then place the ramekins on the napkin. Provide each guest with a salad fork and a small spoon.

Making Omelets

There are three basic types of omelets: rolled, flat, and souffléed. All are made from beaten eggs cooked so that the exterior is firm and smooth while the inside remains somewhere between runny and barely moist. Unlike most egg dishes, omelets are cooked over high heat. The classic omelet, known as a French omelet, is rolled or folded, typically around some type of savory filling. The flat omelet is made much like a large pancake. Souffléed omelets are made puffy and light by separating the eggs and beating the egg whites until airy and light.

In making omelets, the right pan makes an enormous difference. Purists insist on a special heavy-gauge omelet pan, used solely for omelet making and never washed—it is simply rubbed with soft toweling and a handful of salt. While these pans do produce superior omelets, not many of us have the luxury of a kitchen stocked with single-purpose equipment. In truth, any slope-sided, heavy-based pan with a smooth surface will do. Nonstick pans allow you to reduce the amount of cooking fat.

An omelet is easiest to manage and looks best when prepared in the proper size pan. For a 2-egg omelet, a pan with a 6- to 8-inch diameter is best. A 3- to 5-egg omelet needs an 8- to 9-inch pan, and if you insist on showing off with a 6- to 8-egg omelet, wield a 10- to 12-inch pan. Small is beautiful for French omelets: cutting a large rolled omelet into many servings inevitably results in a sloppy mess. If you do want to attempt a large omelet, try a flat omelet or frittata, 33.

HOW TO MAKE A FRENCH OR ROLLED OMELET

A perfectly executed omelet requires a certain practiced rhythm. The eggs should be beaten only enough to thoroughly blend the whites and yolks, not enough to incorporate air or make them frothy.

1 Add the eggs to the hot pan the moment the butter's bubbling begins to subside but before it starts to brown. Grasp the handle of the pan and shake the eggs back and forth while stirring the eggs with your other hand. The best tool for stirring is a table fork, held flat so it does not touch the pan bottom. In as little as 20 to 30 seconds, the eggs will begin to form curds and set firmly along the bottom, while the surface will remain moist. This is your cue to stop stirring and, with the back of the fork, shape the omelet into a neat circle by gently spreading the eggs evenly around the pan. With the surface still moist, quickly add any filling you might want.

2 Roll the omelet with what can be described as a soft fold. Tilt the pan away from you at about a 45-degree angle and use the fork to coax the top third of the omelet away from the handle and down over onto itself (and the filling if there is one). If you prefer an omelet with a lightly browned surface, let the omelet sit for a few seconds on the burner.

3 With a warm plate waiting, slant the pan to 90 degrees or more. Make a second fold by sliding the omelet out of the pan until it falls seam side down on the plate. Straighten the edges of the omelet to form a neat oval and serve immediately.

French Omelet

1 serving

The success of any omelet demands that the fat in the pan be hot enough to gently set the exterior of the omelet at once, but not so hot as to toughen it before the rest of the egg cooks. With the pan at the proper heat, a 2-egg omelet takes less than 1 ½ minutes to cook from the time the beaten egg hits the hot pan until the finished omelet is rolled out onto a warmed plate. Have all your ingredients ready when you start cooking. When making more than one omelet, beat the total number of eggs, and use a ladle or measuring cup to pour 3½ ounces, or a scant ¼ cup, for each 2-egg omelet. Keep melted butter and filling ingredients by the stove and move quickly, making the omelets one by one. Serve them as they are ready, or keep them warm in a 200°F oven and serve when all are finished. If making more than four, use another pan or two. Attention to more than one pan at a time is a skill that needs to be developed. Stagger the different pans' "schedules" so that the omelets are not all at the same stage at once.

Combine and beat with a fork until the whites and yolks are blended:

2 large eggs
Scant ⅛ teaspoon salt
Pinch of ground black pepper

Melt in a 6- to 8-inch skillet over medium-high heat:

1 tablespoon butter

Tilt the skillet to coat the sides and bottom thoroughly. When the butter is hot and the foam has subsided, pour in the eggs. Shake the pan back and forth while stirring the eggs with your other hand, using a fork held flat, just above the pan bottom. If adding a filling, do so once the bottom has set, placing it in a line in the center of the omelet. Use the fork to begin to roll the edge of the omelet toward the center, all the while tilting the pan to fold the omelet against the pan wall. Check if the underside of the omelet is as browned as you wish. If not, leave on the heat for a few seconds more before serving. With a warmed plate at the ready, tilt the pan up until the omelet makes a second fold and slips seam side down onto the plate.

FILLING OMELETS

An omelet's filling should complement the delicate flavor of the eggs, not overwhelm it. The classic French omelet is sometimes made with only eggs and salt and pepper; ingredients such as chopped herbs and finely diced meats may be added directly to the beaten eggs, while more substantial fillings may be placed in the middle of the omelet just before it is rolled up. To fill a 2-egg omelet, have ready ⅓ to ½ cup of filling. Place 2 tablespoons in the omelet while it is still in the pan and before you have rolled it, aiming for a line along the middle third. Reserve the remainder for a final garnish on top. Or fold the omelet without a filling and then, after it is on the plate, cut an incision along the top and fill it with the warm garnish. Fillings should be fully cooked (if cooking is necessary at all) and neither too cold nor too hot when added to an omelet.

FOLDED OMELET

1 serving

For a beginner, the firmer texture of this omelet is a bit more manageable. It is neatly folded in half and does not require the tricky shaking and stirring action of the French omelet.

Prepare *French Omelet, left,* using 2 eggs and adding 2 tablespoons milk, cream, or stock to the beaten eggs. As the omelet cooks, instead of stirring and shaking the pan, lift the edges of the omelet with a pancake turner and tilt the skillet to allow the uncooked egg mixture to run to the bottom. When all is an even consistency, place any filling on the bottom half and fold the omelet in half, forming a half-moon shape. Serve immediately on a warmed plate.

EGG-WHITE OMELET

1 serving

For anyone on a low-cholesterol, reduced-fat diet, it is possible to modify egg recipes to eliminate the yolks. Since the yolks carry the richness and flavor of the egg, we recommend compensating by adding more in the way of your favorite seasonings and fillings.

Prepare *Folded Omelet, above,* substituting 3 egg whites for the 2 whole eggs, eliminating the milk, cream, or stock, and using vegetable oil in place of butter. Add chopped herbs and plenty of seasonings to the whites before adding them to the pan. Choose a moist, zesty filling.

Savory Cheese and Herb-Filled Souffléed Omelet

4 servings

This impressive creation is made by separating eggs and beating the whites until stiff, as you would for a soufflé. The omelet is then cooked in an omelet pan until puffy and light and can be either left flat or folded over to envelop a filling. We especially like sweet fillings, such as fruit or preserves, with these omelets, but savory cheese or herb fillings can also be delicious. Whatever your choice, do not overdo it. Use no more than ⅓ cup prepared fruit or a few tablespoons of jam thinned with a teaspoon of liquor for 4 eggs. A properly executed souffléed omelet has a lovely brown, firm, dry exterior enveloping a soft, creamy, airy center. With the added volume of the beaten whites,
you get more servings from fewer eggs, and 1 egg per person satisfies most appetites.

Preheat the oven to 375°F.

Combine and whisk until thick and light:

4 large egg yolks

Salt and ground black pepper to taste

In a separate bowl, beat until stiff but not dry:

4 large egg whites

Pinch of salt

Fold the yolk mixture gently into the whites. Melt in a 10-inch ovenproof skillet over medium heat:

1 to 2 tablespoons butter

When the foam has subsided, pour
the batter into the pan, spread evenly, and smooth the top. Shake the pan after a few seconds to discourage sticking and then cover the pan with a lid whose underside has been buttered to prevent sticking. Reduce the heat and cook for about 5 minutes. Remove the cover and sprinkle the top of the omelet with:

2 tablespoons chopped herbs (chives, parsley, chervil, or a combination)

¼ cup grated cheese

Place the skillet in the oven until the top is set, 3 to 5 minutes. Either fold the omelet in half or slide it out onto a warmed plate and serve with:

Tomato sauce or *Salsa Verde Cruda*, 49

Tortilla Española (Potato Omelet)

6 servings

In the United States, a Spanish omelet is a rolled one filled with peppers and tomatoes—but this authentic Spanish version is flat (but usually thick) and filled with potatoes and onions. Tortilla means "little cake" but in this case has nothing to do with the little cakes of corn or wheat flour called tortillas in Mexico and Central America.

Heat in a large skillet over medium heat:

2 tablespoons olive oil

Add:

1 large onion (about 8 ounces), cut into ⅛-inch-thick slices

Salt and ground black pepper to taste

Cook until the onions are soft and golden, reducing the heat as they cook, about 20 minutes. Remove to a large bowl. Heat in the same skillet over high heat:

¼ cup olive oil

Add:

1 pound red-skinned potatoes, peeled and cut into ⅛-inch-thick slices

Cook until golden brown, 10 to 12 minutes. Reduce the heat to medium-high if the oil gets too hot and smoky. Toss the potatoes often with a metal spatula, separating the slices that stick together. Some will stick together no matter what you do, and that is fine. Remove the potatoes with a slotted spoon to paper towels to drain. Set aside the pan with the oil in it. Add to the onions and mix together:

6 large eggs

½ teaspoon salt

Ground black pepper to taste

Sprinkle the potatoes with:

Salt and ground black pepper to taste

Add the potatoes to the egg mixture and toss to coat the slices well with the eggs. Return the skillet to high heat to heat the remaining oil in the pan. When hot, add the egg mixture and immediately reduce the heat to low. Let the omelet cook for 3 to 4 minutes, undisturbed, until the bottom is golden and the eggs are two-thirds to three-quarters set. Shake the pan from time to time to make sure the omelet does not stick. If it does, slide a metal spatula under the omelet to free it from the pan and continue cooking. Place a lightly oiled large heatproof plate upside down over the omelet and flip the skillet to turn the omelet over. Slide the omelet back into the pan to cook the second side. Cook until golden and set, 2 to 3 minutes more. Shake the omelet loose from the pan and slide onto a clean plate. Cut into 6 wedges and serve hot or at room temperature.

Onion Frittata with Sherry Vinegar Sauce

4 to 6 servings

In flat omelets, eggs assume a supporting role, binding the ingredients and adding richness while the emphasis is on the filling. A flat omelet can be thick or thin, but it is always too hearty and awkward to roll or fold; instead, it is served in wedges, much like an open-faced pizza. Flat omelets can be made ahead and served at room temperature.

Caramelize, 46:

1½ pounds onions

Just before removing from the heat, season with:

1 tablespoon sherry vinegar

Plenty of ground black pepper

Preheat the broiler.

Beat with a fork just to combine:

5 large eggs

½ teaspoon salt

2 tablespoons chopped fresh parsley

Stir in the onions. Melt in a medium, ovenproof, nonstick skillet over medium heat:

1 tablespoon butter

When the butter foams, swirl it around the pan, then pour in the eggs. Shake the pan back and forth a few times to loosen the bottom, then turn the heat down to medium-low, cover, and cook until the eggs are set and well colored on the bottom, about 10 minutes. Uncover and place under the broiler. When the frittata is set and nicely browned on top, slide it onto a serving plate. Return the pan to medium heat.

Add:

1 tablespoon butter

When the butter foams, pour in:

1 tablespoon sherry vinegar

Rapidly shake the pan back and forth to combine.

Spoon the sauce over the eggs, then serve.

Quiche Lorraine

One 9-inch quiche; 4 to 6 servings

This brunch and lunch classic is a specialty of the Lorraine region of northeastern France, where it was first made as early as the sixteenth century. Traditional quiche Lorraine contains no cheese.

Prepare:

Flaky Pastry Dough, below

Roll out the dough and fit it into a 9-inch quiche, tart, or pie pan. Refrigerate the crust for at least 30 minutes.

Position the rack in the lower third of the oven. Preheat the oven to 400°F.

Smooth a sheet of heavy-duty aluminum foil, shiny side down, over the bottom and sides of the crust, flaring the excess foil, like an awning, over the crust edge to keep it from overbrowning. Fill the liner with raw beans or rice or metal pie weights, banking the weights against the sides of the crust if you do not have enough to fill the crust to the brim. Bake the crust for 20 minutes with the weights in place to set the pastry. Carefully lift out the foil with the weights inside. Prick the crust thoroughly with a fork, return it to the oven and bake until the crust is golden brown all over, 5 to 10 minutes more. Check the crust periodically; if it puffs along the bottom, prick it with a fork, then press down gently with the back of a spoon. Whisk together, then brush the inside with:

1 large egg yolk
Pinch of salt

Return to the oven until the egg glaze sets, 1 to 2 minutes.

Reduce the oven temperature to 375°F.

Cook in a heavy skillet over medium heat, stirring constantly, until the fat is almost rendered but the bacon is not yet crisp:

**4 ounces sliced bacon, cut into
    1-inch pieces**

Drain on paper towels. Beat together:

3 large eggs, lightly beaten
**1½ cups crème fraîche, heavy
    cream, or half-and-half**
½ teaspoon salt
¼ teaspoon ground black pepper
**Pinch of freshly grated or
    ground nutmeg**

Arrange the bacon on the bottom of the crust and pour the custard into it. Bake until the filling is browned and set, 25 to 35 minutes.

Flaky Pastry Dough

One 9-inch pie crust

Using a rubber spatula, thoroughly mix in a large bowl:

1¼ cups all-purpose flour
**½ teaspoon white sugar, or
    1½ teaspoons powdered sugar**
½ teaspoon salt

Add:

**½ cup solid vegetable shortening,
    or ¼ cup shortening and
    4 tablespoons (½ stick) cold
    unsalted butter**

Break the shortening into large chunks; if using butter, cut into small pieces, then add to the flour mixture. Cut the fat into the dry ingredients by chopping vigorously with a pastry blender or by cutting in with 2 knives. Periodically stir dry flour up from the bottom of the bowl and scrape clinging fat off the pastry blender or knives. Some of the fat should remain in pea-sized pieces; the rest should be reduced to the consistency of coarse crumbs. The mixture should seem dry and powdery, not pasty or greasy. Drizzle over the flour and fat mixture:

3 tablespoons ice water

Using the rubber spatula, cut with the blade side until the mixture looks evenly moistened and begins to form small balls. Press down on the dough with the flat side of the spatula. If the balls of dough stick together, you have added enough water; if they do not, drizzle over the top:

1 tablespoon ice water

Cut in the water, again using the blade of the spatula, then press with your hands until the dough coheres. The dough should look rough, not smooth. Press the dough into a round flat disk and wrap tightly in plastic. Refrigerate for at least 30 minutes—preferably for several hours—for up to 2 days before rolling. The dough can also be wrapped airtight and frozen for up to 6 months; thaw completely before rolling.

Leek Tart (Flamiche aux Poireaux)

One 9-inch tart; 6 servings

This is a rich leek and cream pie from northern France.

Prepare:

Flaky Pastry Dough, opposite

Roll out the dough ⅛ inch thick and fit into a buttered 9-inch quiche, tart, or pie pan. Refrigerate while you prepare the filling.

Melt in a medium skillet over medium heat:

2 tablespoons unsalted butter

Add:

2 pounds leeks, trimmed to white and tender green parts only, split lengthwise, cleaned thoroughly, and cut into ¼-inch-thick slices (about 4 cups)

½ teaspoon salt

Ground black pepper to taste

Cover and cook until the leeks are very soft, with little color, stirring occasionally and reducing the heat as they cook, about 30 minutes. After about 15 minutes of cooking time, set a rack in the lowest position in the oven. Preheat the oven to 400°F.

For the custards, beat together until well combined:

2 large eggs

½ cup heavy cream, half-and-half, or light cream

¼ teaspoon freshly grated or ground nutmeg

Salt and ground black pepper to taste

Remove the pastry shell from the refrigerator. When the leeks are done, add to the custard and transfer to the prepared pastry shell. Bake until golden and the custard is set, 20 to 30 minutes. Let rest for 10 minutes to settle, then cut into wedges and serve.

LEEKS

Leeks are a member of the onion family. Leeks are in season from fall to spring, but they are in the market most of the year. When buying a bunch, try to choose leeks all the same size, preferably small. Be sure the leaves are bright, crisp, and not torn and the white parts are not discolored. The layers of a leek can contain dirt, since the white stalks are "blanched," buried in earth to keep them pale. Swish sliced leeks in a large bowl of cool water. Let them stand a few minutes while the dirt falls to the bottom, then lift them out with a strainer. Repeat if there is a lot of dirt left in the bowl. Store in perforated plastic vegetable bags in the refrigerator crisper.

Basic Breakfast Strata

6 to 8 servings

Sausage, cheese, vegetables, or whatever strikes your fancy gives this bread-based strata character and flavor. It can be left in the refrigerator overnight to meld, and baked the next morning while the coffee brews.

Butter a 2½-quart soufflé dish or casserole. Heat a large, heavy skillet over medium-high heat and add:

1½ pounds bulk *Country* or *Breakfast Sausage*, 38, or store-bought sausage

Brown the sausage for 5 minutes, breaking it up with a fork as it cooks. Add:

2 cups sliced mushrooms

½ cup finely chopped onions

Cook for 5 minutes, stirring frequently. Set aside. In a large bowl, combine:

4 large eggs, lightly beaten

2 cups milk

Have ready:

1 large loaf day-old Italian bread, cut into 18 to 20 slices, crusts removed, buttered if desired

Layer one-third of the bread in the bottom of the prepared baking dish. Top with half of the sausage mixture and sprinkle with one-third of:

1½ cups grated Swiss or Cheddar cheese

Repeat with another layer of bread, the other half of the sausage, and another ½ cup cheese. Cover with a third layer of bread. Slowly pour the milk and egg mixture over the top and sprinkle with the last ½ cup grated cheese. Let the strata stand for at least 1 hour or cover and refrigerate for up to 24 hours.

Preheat the oven to 350°F.

Set a baking sheet on the lowest rack of the oven to catch any drips and bake the strata until the top is nicely browned and bubbly, about 1 hour.

ABOUT **SIDE** DISHES

We love this grab-bag chapter for the ease and speed with which most of its dishes, elegant or plebeian, may be prepared.

Many of the recipes on the following pages feature meat or seafood. Some of these, like Corned Beef Hash, 41, or Crabcakes, 42, can star on their own at a special-occasion brunch or breakfast. Others provide classic robust accompaniments to breakfast egg dishes.

Even more of the recipes in this chapter are strictly side dishes commonly served along with eggs. But what a marvelous variety they bring to the morning table! From classic Hash Brown Potatoes, 45, to Fried Green Tomatoes, 47, and Mushroom Ragout, 48, they provide hosts and hostesses with a wealth of creativity for entertaining.

Clockwise from left: *Sautéed Ham Steak, 39; Hash Brown Potatoes, 45; Orange-Hazelnut Asparagus, 47*

Country or Breakfast Sausage

2 pounds

Fresh, raw sausages are best slowly pan-fried, or poached or simmered and then grilled or broiled.

Cut into strips if using a meat grinder or 1-inch dice if using a food processor:

1½ pounds pork butt

8 ounces pork fatback, trimmed of rind

Grind the meat and fat together in the meat grinder fitted with a ¼-inch plate, or coarsely chop in the food processor. Mix together in a large bowl with:

2 teaspoons salt

2 teaspoons coarsely ground black pepper

1½ teaspoons dried sage

½ teaspoon dried marjoram

¼ teaspoon dried savory, crumbled

⅛ teaspoon ground ginger

Pinch of ground cloves

Pinch of ground red pepper

¼ cup cold water

Using your hands, knead and squeeze the mixture until well blended. Leave in bulk or form into patties as needed. If not used immediately, fresh sausage can be frozen for up to 2 months.

MAKING SAUSAGE AT HOME

It is quite easy to make fresh, country-style (without casings) homemade sausage patties, especially with a food processor. The advantage of making your own sausage is that you control everything: the freshness, the amount of fat and salt, the quality and type of meat, the spice blend—the ultimate flavor.

When making sausage at home, remember these rules for safety and hygiene:

- Do not taste the raw meat mixture; instead, fry a small patty and taste that to check the seasonings.
- Keep the meat refrigerated before and between all steps.
- Do not leave any meat sitting in the grinder. Wash all utensils and equipment at once, even if you are only going to take a short break.
- Wash your hands frequently.
- If fresh sausage will not be eaten within 3 days, freeze it.

Chicken and Apple Sausage

About 2 pounds

This sausage can be used as a substitute for Country or Breakfast Sausage, above. Although it has less than half the fat of conventional breakfast sausage, it remains juicy if it is not overcooked. One of our favorite ways to serve these sausages is with French Toast, 58, smothered with Buttered Apple Slices, 56.

In a small pan, boil down to 2 to 3 tablespoons syrup:

1 cup apple cider

Remove the bones from:

2¼ pounds chicken thighs

Cut the chicken into strips if using a meat grinder or 1-inch dice if using a food processor. Grind the chicken and skin together in a meat grinder fitted with a ⅜-inch plate, or coarsely chop by hand or in a food processor along with:

1½ ounces dried apples

Mix the chicken and apple mixture and syrup in a large bowl with:

2½ teaspoons salt

1 teaspoon ground black pepper

1 teaspoon dried sage

½ teaspoon dried thyme

⅛ teaspoon ground cinnamon

⅛ teaspoon ground ginger

Using your hands, knead and squeeze the mixture until well blended. Leave in bulk or form into patties as needed. If not used immediately, fresh sausage can be frozen for up to 2 months.

Sautéed Ham Steak

4 servings

Melt in a large skillet over medium-high heat:

1½ teaspoons unsalted butter

Add:

1 fully cooked ¾- to 1-inch-thick ham steak (1½ to 2 pounds)

Sauté the steak until nicely browned, 3 to 5 minutes each side. Remove to a platter and season with:

Ground black pepper to taste

HAM STEAK WITH RED-EYE GRAVY

Prepare *Sautéed Ham Steak, left,* cutting the slices ¼ to ½ inch thick. After the ham is cooked, remove it to a warmed platter and return the skillet to the heat. Add 1 cup of brewed coffee and boil, stirring, until it turns slightly red. Add ½ cup of heavy cream, reduce the heat, and simmer until slightly thickened, about 10 minutes. Season with salt and ground black pepper to taste.

HAM, BACON, AND CANADIAN BACON

The term *ham* is used for a variety of pork cuts from either the back leg or front shoulder that are processed through salt-curing and sometimes smoking and aging.

Ham is usually labeled one of two ways: "Partially Cooked" or "Fully Cooked." Whichever you buy, follow scrupulously the packer's instructions on the label. Partially cooked hams—also labeled "Cook Before Eating"—need to be roasted to an internal temperature of 155° to 160°F. Fully cooked hams—also called "Ready to Eat" or "Ready to Serve"—can be eaten as is.

Both partially and fully cooked hams come in several sizes and shapes. The whole ham, a 10- to 15-pound hind leg of pork with bone intact, is the most flavorful and least wasteful cut. For smaller meals, you can buy a section of the whole ham, either the rounded part called the rump half, or butt portion. The rump half is somewhat more meaty but relatively difficult to carve. Smaller steaks and ham roasts are also available cut from the center of the leg.

Bacon is made from trimmed hog bellies, also called sides, that have been cured in brine and then smoked until partially cooked. Bacon is a fatty cut, and although there are leaner varieties, the fat that remains is integral to its flavor and texture. Most bacon is sliced—thick or thin. Bacon loses flavor with time and should be used within a week or so of purchase. It can be frozen, but only for one or two months. When cooking bacon under the broiler or in a skillet, start with a cold grill or pan to prevent curling. Do not cook bacon over high heat, since it can go from browned to burnt in a matter of seconds. Separating slices of bacon in the pan as it warms helps prevent tearing of individual slices.

Canadian bacon bears little resemblance to standard bacon, because it comes from the meatier, leaner loin of the pig and is more thoroughly trimmed before curing. Although most Canadian bacon is brined and smoked and closely resembles ham, it is also sold uncooked. Slice the cooked variety as you would regular ham.

Basic Pan-Broiled Steak

4 servings

Pan-broiling, or dry-skillet cooking, is a simple and convenient method for cooking any steak up to 2 inches thick. It is especially useful for steaks less than ¾ inch thick, which fare poorly if grilled or broiled. As an added advantage, pan-broiling is an excellent method for achieving a good crisp crust. It is important to get the pan hot enough that the meat sizzles the instant it hits the pan: lower temperatures will not produce the desired crust. The only disadvantage is that the high heat used for pan-broiling creates smoke and splattering, but this problem can be easily solved by opening a window or turning on the kitchen exhaust fan.

Pat dry:

4 small beef steaks (6 to 12 ounces each) or 2 larger steaks (¾ to 1½ pounds each), ¾ to 1½ inches thick

If the meat is very lean, brush it with:

Olive oil

Season both sides of the steaks with:

Salt and ground black pepper to taste

Heat a large, heavy skillet or griddle over medium-high heat. You may need 2 skillets if the steaks are large. To determine when the pan is hot enough, touch a corner of the steak to the pan; it should sizzle briskly. Once the pan is hot, sear the steaks on one side, without crowding, for about 5 minutes. Turn them over and sear the other side for 3 to 4 minutes for rare, 5 to 8 minutes for medium. You may need to turn the steak more than once if one side gets too brown before the steak is done. Pour off any fat that accumulates during cooking.

PAN-BROILING STEAK

Pan-broiling is best done in a well-seasoned heavy skillet or griddle or nonstick skillet. Specially designed ridged cast-iron pans are ideal but not necessary. Steaks should be patted dry and seasoned well with salt and pepper immediately before cooking: salting too far in advance makes the surface too moist for the meat to brown evenly. Do not hold back on seasoning: pan-broiling is the technique used to produce spicy "blackened" steaks. With a well-seasoned pan, additional oil or fat is unnecessary when cooking well-marbled steaks. For leaner cuts, we recommend a light coating of vegetable oil. Do not overcrowd the pan. Cook steaks uncovered, turning them occasionally. Pour off any fat that accumulates to keep from frying the steaks.

Sautéed Bacon

When cooking bacon, cook to personal taste; the longer bacon cooks, the more fat is rendered out of it. Count on about 2 or 3 slices bacon per person.

Place in a large cast-iron or other heavy skillet:

2 or 3 slices bacon per person

Do not overlap the slices; cook in batches if necessary. Place the pan over medium-low heat and slowly cook the bacon until browned. Turn the bacon often and monitor the heat to avoid burning the bacon. Spoon off the fat if over ¼ inch accumulates in the pan during cooking. Remove the slices to paper towels to drain.

Sautéed Canadian Bacon

Canadian bacon is boneless pork loin that has been brine-cured and smoked.

Melt in a large skillet over medium heat:

1½ teaspoons butter or vegetable oil

Add:

2 or 3 slices Canadian bacon per person, ⅛ to ¼ inch thick

Cook the slices, turning often, until browned and heated through, 3 to 5 minutes. Remove to plates and serve.

Corned Beef Hash

4 to 6 servings

The name of this beef is a reference to the corn-sized crystals of salt used to brine large cuts of beef brisket, sometimes with added allspice, black pepper, and bay leaves. The corned beef sold in our markets is still a salt-and-spice brine-cured cut of beef brisket or round. In New England, it is still possible to find a "gray-cured" brisket, referring to the color of corned beef made without chemicals to preserve its rosy color. Corned beef is sold in vacuum-sealed bags that contain some of the brine and seasonings used during curing. It needs to be cooked before serving. New Englanders say that this hash must be put together from the leftovers of New England boiled dinner. However, it can be made quite successfully with corned beef bought from a deli. Ask for a slice that is thick enough to be cut into ½-inch cubes. A well-seasoned cast-iron skillet gives the hash a good brown crust, but a nonstick skillet makes unmolding easy. The quantities and pan size depend on the amount of leftovers you have, but here are approximate measurements.

Add to a large, heavy skillet over medium-high heat:

3 tablespoons vegetable oil

1 cup chopped onions

Cook, stirring, until the onions are lightly browned, about 3 minutes. Add:

3 cups cooked corned beef, cut into ½-inch cubes (about 2 pounds)

2 to 3 cups cooked potatoes, cut into ½-inch cubes

RED FLANNEL HASH

Beets give this hash its color and its name.

Prepare *Corned Beef Hash*, left, adding 2 or 3 beets, cooked, peeled, and cut into ½-inch cubes, to the other vegetables.

Stir once, reduce the heat to medium, and press down with a spatula to compress the hash. Cook, without disturbing, until the bottom is well browned, 10 to 15 minutes. Slide or invert the hash onto a serving plate. Garnish with:

Chopped fresh parsley

Serve with:

Poached Eggs, 26, or fried eggs

Crabcakes

4 servings

Buy fresh lump crabmeat and give your-self time to refrigerate the cakes after you shape them so that they will hold together better when you cook them.
Gently pick over for bits of shell and cartilage:

1 pound fresh lump crabmeat
In a skillet over medium heat, warm:

2 tablespoons butter or olive oil
When the butter foam has subsided, add:

1 tablespoon finely diced red bell pepper (optional)
½ cup diced scallions
1 teaspoon minced garlic
Cook, stirring, until the mixture is tender but not browned, about 10 minutes. Set aside. In a large bowl, mix the crabmeat with:

1 egg, lightly beaten
¼ cup mayonnaise
1 tablespoon Dijon mustard

Salt and ground black pepper to taste
¼ teaspoon ground red pepper (optional)
¼ cup minced fresh parsley, cilantro, or dill
2 tablespoons fresh breadcrumbs, toasted
Add the sautéed vegetables and blend well. Place on a plate:

1 to 2 cups fresh breadcrumbs, toasted
Shape the crab mixture into 8 small or 4 large cakes and, 1 at a time, coat each of the cakes in the bread-crumbs, pressing lightly to make sure the crumbs coat evenly. Place the cakes on a rack, or on a plate covered with wax paper, and refrig-erate for 1 to 2 hours if you have the time. When you are ready to cook, heat in a large skillet over medium heat:

¼ cup butter, *Clarified Butter*, 27, or oil
When the fat is hot, add the cakes, 1 at a time; do not crowd—it is fine to cook them in two batches. Adjust the heat so that the fat is sizzling but not burning the breadcrumbs. Rotate the cakes from side to side once or twice so that they brown evenly before turning them over after about 5 minutes. Cook until both sides are nicely browned; smaller cakes need a total of 8 to 10 minutes of cooking, larger ones 12 to 15 minutes. Keep any finished cakes warm in a 300°F oven while you complete the cooking. Serve hot with:

Lemon wedges or *Salsa Verde Cruda*, 49 (*opposite*)

Salmon Croquettes

4 servings

Combine in a medium bowl:
1 pound cooked or canned salmon
1½ cups mashed potatoes
¼ cup heavy cream
1 tablespoon chopped fresh parsley
1 teaspoon snipped fresh chives
1 teaspoon snipped fresh dill
¼ teaspoon ground red pepper
Salt to taste
Spread in separate shallow bowls:
2 cups fresh breadcrumbs
2 cups all-purpose flour
Whisk together in a third shallow bowl:
4 large eggs

Shape the salmon mixture into 8 patties. Working with 1 patty at a time, coat lightly with the flour and shake off the excess. Dip quickly into the eggs and let the excess drip off, then coat with the breadcrumbs. Heat in a large nonstick skillet over medium heat until sizzling:
2 tablespoons unsalted butter
Add as many of the croquettes as will fit comfortably. Cook until golden on both sides, about 2 minutes each side. Remove and repeat with the remaining croquettes.

BUYING FISH

Buy fish from a market where you can see and smell the fish easily. Never buy fish that is not stored at 33°F. It should be on ice or in a refrigerated case with a thermome-ter. Good fish has firm, unmarred flesh and smells like fresh seawater. The surface of the fish should be bright, clear, and almost translucent. It should not have spots of pink (bruises) or brown (spoilage), and it should have no areas of deep red or brown.

Pommes Anna

6 to 8 servings

Position a rack in the center of the oven. Preheat the oven to 425°F. Have ready:

12 tablespoons (1½ sticks) butter, clarified, 27

Pour the butter into a Pommes Anna pan (opposite) or an 8-inch cast-iron skillet to a depth of ¼ inch. Set over low heat and layer in:

2½ to 3 pounds potatoes, preferably Yukon gold, peeled and sliced ⅛ inch thick

Build the bottom layer especially carefully with overlapping, nicely shaped slices. As you assemble the slices, sprinkle each layer with:

Salt and ground black pepper to taste

Melted butter (optional)

When all the potatoes are in the pan, lightly butter or oil a pot lid slightly smaller than the pan, and press it firmly on top of the potatoes to compress them. Cover the pan and put in the oven over a baking sheet to catch any drips. Bake for 20 minutes, remove the cover, and press down firmly on the potatoes. Bake, uncovered, until the sides are visibly browned and crisp, 20 to 25 minutes more. Holding the lid firmly against the potatoes, tilt the pan and pour off any melted butter that has not been absorbed. To serve, invert the potatoes onto a plate and cut into wedges.

Hash Brown Potatoes

4 servings

There are two kinds of hash browns: those made with raw potatoes and those made with boiled ones. The latter stick together better and cook more quickly, but some prefer the texture of those that begin raw.

Toss together:

1½ pounds boiled or raw all-purpose potatoes, peeled and finely diced (about 4 cups)

2 tablespoons finely chopped onions (optional)

½ teaspoon salt

Ground black pepper to taste

Heat in a large, heavy skillet over medium-high heat:

3 tablespoons vegetable oil

Add the potatoes, toss them a few times, then spread them evenly in the pan and press down with a spatula. Reduce the heat to medium and cook slowly, pressing down several more times, until browned on the bottom, about 15 minutes. As the potatoes cook, give the pan a gentle shake a few times to make sure they are not sticking. Cut the cake down the middle, then, using 2 spatulas, turn each side over. Do not worry if they do not turn evenly. If the pan seems too dry, add a little more oil before you return the potatoes. Cook the second side until golden brown. Serve piping hot.

Golden Potato Pancakes (Rösti)

2 or 3 servings

Rösti, the classic Swiss potato pancake, can be made with raw or boiled potatoes.

Toss together:

1 pound all-purpose potatoes, cooked, peeled, and coarsely grated, or 1 pound raw all-purpose potatoes, peeled, cut into thin strips, rinsed, and dried

½ teaspoon salt

Melt in a medium, heavy skillet over medium heat:

2 tablespoons butter

Add the potatoes and cook for 4 to 5 minutes, turning frequently so that the shreds are all lightly coated with butter. Press together to form a cake, reduce the heat to low, and cook until golden on the bottom, about 20 minutes. Turn the cake out onto a plate, then slide it back into the pan and cook the second side. If desired, sprinkle the top with:

1½ tablespoons grated Gruyère cheese

When the second side is golden, slide the potato cake onto a serving plate. Cut into 2 or 3 pieces and serve plain or garnished with:

Snipped fresh chives

Caramelized Onions

About 4 cups

If you cook onions over low heat so that they wilt without browning, they are said to be sweated. At this stage, their taste is gentle but not sweet. If you continue cooking, the onions will caramelize, or turn brown and quite sweet. The onions cook down to about half their volume and can be refrigerated for a few days or frozen.

Heat in a very large skillet until the butter is melted:

2 tablespoons butter
2 tablespoons olive oil

Add:

3 pounds onions, thinly sliced
Sprinkle with:

1 teaspoon salt
Cook over the lowest possible heat for 1 hour, turning the onions several times. Do not be tempted to increase the heat—the onions need to be thoroughly soft before they begin to brown. Once they are soft, increase the heat to medium and cook, stirring constantly, until well browned, or caramelized, about 25 minutes

more. If the residue from the juices has built up in the pan, add:

½ cup dry white wine or water
Scrape the pan to dissolve the browned bits. They will immediately mix into the onions, darkening them further. Remove from the heat and season well with:

Salt and plenty of ground black pepper to taste
If serving as a side dish, you might want to add:

Grated Parmesan cheese

Fried Green Tomatoes

6 servings

Remove the stem ends, then cut crosswise into ½-inch-thick slices:

6 large green tomatoes

Combine in a shallow bowl:

2 cups fine cornmeal
½ cup all-purpose flour
1 tablespoon chopped fresh parsley
1 tablespoon chopped fresh thyme
1 teaspoon paprika
Salt and ground black pepper
   to taste

Dip the tomato slices 1 at a time into:

1 cup milk

Then coat with the cornmeal mixture. Shake off the excess and set on a plate. Heat in a large skillet until hot enough to sizzle a drop of water:

1 cup vegetable oil

Add the tomatoes in a single layer. Fry until golden and crisp, turning once. Repeat with the remaining tomatoes, adding oil as needed.

Kale with Bacon

2 to 4 servings

Strip the leaves from the stems, discard the stems, wash well, and coarsely chop:

1 large bunch kale (about
   1 pound)

Cook in a large skillet until crisp, then remove to paper towels to drain:

1 or 2 slices bacon, diced

Pour off all but 1 tablespoon of the drippings, then add to the skillet:

1 tablespoon olive oil
1 small onion, finely chopped
1 clove garlic, chopped

Cook over medium heat until the onions are golden brown, then add as much kale as will fit in the skillet and sprinkle with:

Salt

When the kale cooks down, add the rest. Cover and cook over medium heat until the kale is tender, 15 to 20 minutes. Season with:

Salt and ground black pepper
   to taste

Toss with the reserved bacon along with:

1 tablespoon red wine vinegar

Orange-Hazelnut Asparagus

4 servings

Steam or boil:

1 pound asparagus, bottoms
   snapped off

Place a large skillet over medium heat and add:

2 tablespoons butter
1½ tablespoons grated orange zest
¼ cup chopped hazelnuts, toasted

Juice of ½ orange

Cook until the butter is slightly browned, then add the cooked asparagus. Toss several times to heat through, then add:

Salt and ground black pepper
   to taste

Mushroom Ragout

4 servings

For more intense flavor, soak ½ ounce dried mushrooms, chop, and add with the fresh mushrooms; use the soaking water for part of the liquid.

Heat over medium-high heat in a large saucepan:

1 tablespoon olive oil

Add and cook until golden, about 10 minutes:

1 onion, diced

Remove and set aside. Heat in the same pan over medium heat:

1 tablespoon olive oil

Add and cook until they begin to release their liquid:

**1 pound assorted fresh mush-
rooms, wiped clean and
thickly sliced**

Add the onions along with:

2 cloves garlic, finely chopped

**1 teaspoon chopped fresh rose-
mary, or scant ½ teaspoon dried**

**Salt and cracked black peppercorns
to taste**

Cook until the mushrooms begin to brown, another 3 to 4 minutes. Stir in:

1 tablespoon tomato paste

Increase the heat to high and cook, stirring, for 1 to 2 minutes more. Add:

**1½ cups vegetable stock, chicken
stock, or water**

Reduce the heat and simmer for 10 minutes. Stir in to form a sauce:

**2 tablespoons cold butter, cut
into pieces**

1½ teaspoons balsamic vinegar

Garnish with:

Grated Parmesan cheese (optional)

Chopped fresh parsley

Becker Duxelles

About 1 cup

This mushroom flavoring is delicious on toast, in scrambled eggs, or in omelets.

Chop very fine or pulse in a food processor until they resemble coarse sand:

8 ounces mushrooms, wiped clean

Squeeze about ¼ cup of the mushrooms at a time in dampened cheesecloth or a thin cotton towel and wring them very hard to extract their bitter juices. The mushrooms will be in a solid lump if you have squeezed hard enough. Heat in a medium skillet until the foam subsides:

2 tablespoons butter

3 tablespoons olive oil

Add and cook briefly over medium heat until translucent:

½ cup very finely chopped onions

2 cloves garlic, minced

Add the mushrooms and cook, stirring often, over medium-high heat until they have begun to brown and there is very little liquid, 5 to 6 minutes. Stir in:

2 tablespoons port or dry red wine

½ teaspoon ground black pepper

¼ teaspoon grated lemon zest

Cook until completely evaporated. Add:

¼ cup heavy cream (optional)

Salt to taste

**Pinch of dried thyme or grated or
ground nutmeg**

Let cool, then refrigerate in a covered container for up to 10 days or freeze for up to 3 months.

MUSHROOMS

Mushrooms lend both elegance and earthiness to a dish. While we are grateful for the abundance of cultivated small button mushrooms, wild mushrooms have considerably more character, and an assortment of them is available in specialty groceries and supermarkets. Choose mushrooms that are heavy for their size, with dry, firm caps and stems—nothing damp or shriveled, no dark or soft spots, and all close to the same size. If the gills are open, the mushrooms are more mature and their flavor will be stronger, and with a wild mushroom, this may be a plus. Open-gilled mushrooms should be used as soon as possible.

Wrap unwashed mushrooms in a loosely closed paper bag or wrap loosely in damp paper towels. Leave packaged mushrooms in their unopened package. Store on a refrigerator shelf, not in the crisper.

Clean mushrooms with a soft brush or wipe with a damp cloth. Or if the mushrooms are truly grimy, rinse them quickly under cold running water and pat dry.

Ratatouille

4 to 6 servings

This Provençal vegetable mélange can be served chilled with a splash of lemon juice or herb vinegar.

Sauté in a large skillet or Dutch oven over high heat until the vegetables are golden and just tender, 10 to 12 minutes:

¼ cup olive oil

1 medium eggplant (about 1 pound), peeled and cut into 1-inch cubes

1 pound zucchini, cut into 1-inch cubes

Remove the vegetables and reduce the heat to medium-high. In the same pan, cook until the onions are slightly softened:

2 tablespoons olive oil

1½ cups sliced onions

Add and cook, stirring occasionally, until the vegetables are just tender but not browned, 8 to 12 minutes:

2 large red bell peppers, cut into 1-inch squares

3 cloves garlic, chopped

Season with:

Salt and ground black pepper to taste

Add:

1½ cups chopped seeded peeled fresh tomatoes

2 or 3 sprigs fresh thyme

1 bay leaf

Reduce the heat to low, cover, and cook for 5 minutes. Add the eggplant and zucchini and cook until everything is tender, about 20 minutes more. Taste and adjust the seasonings. Stir in:

¼ cup chopped fresh basil

Corn Pudding Cockaigne

4 servings

For variation, add a little chopped fresh tarragon, thyme, basil, or mint.

Preheat the oven to 325°F. Butter an 8 x 8-inch baking dish.

Cut and scrape the kernels from:

4 ears sweet corn (about 2 cups)

Combine with:

½ to ¾ cup heavy cream

1 teaspoon sugar (optional)

Salt and ground white pepper to taste

Spread the corn mixture in the baking dish. Dot the top with:

1 tablespoon butter, cut into small pieces

Bake until the pudding is set, 30 to 40 minutes.

PREPARING CORN

To remove kernels from the cob, hold the ear firmly with the bottom end placed in a shallow soup bowl to keep the kernels from splattering. Cut straight down the cob with a sharp knife, cutting two or three rows at a time.

Salsa Verde Cruda

About 2 cups

Intensely fresh, pungent, and herbal, this salsa is the easiest of all. It is especially good with eggs. Tomatillos, picked underripe, have a lemony tang that lends sprightliness to sauces in Mexican cooking. Since the onion is not rinsed and everything is whirled to a puree, the salsa must be served within an hour of preparing for optimum quality. If left to sit, the raw onion will overpower the sauce.

Combine in a food processor or blender and coarsely puree, leaving the mixture a little chunky:

8 ounces tomatillos, husked, rinsed, and coarsely chopped

1 small white or red onion, coarsely chopped

3 to 5 fresh green chili peppers (such as serrano or jalapeño), seeded and coarsely chopped

1 clove garlic, peeled (optional)

3 to 4 tablespoons fresh cilantro sprigs

Remove to a medium bowl and stir in enough cold water to loosen the mixture to a saucelike consistency. Stir in:

1 teaspoon salt, or to taste

¾ teaspoon sugar (optional)

Serve immediately.

ABOUT **PANCAKES,** WAFFLES, FRENCH TOAST & DOUGHNUTS

*P*erhaps no foods lend themselves to more occasions than those in this chapter. Not only can they all be served as breakfast or brunch main courses, but many may also be served as hors d'oeuvres, as luncheon or supper treats, or as desserts.

Many people like to cook pancakes, waffles, or French toast at table, using auxiliary heat so that they reach guests in peak condition. Waffle irons, electric skillets, or a double crêpe pan set, on which crêpes can be both cooked and sauced, are all tableside conveniences. In the kitchen, both cast-iron and nonstick griddles have their adherents.

No matter what your source of heat, be it a hot rock, an electric skillet, or an automatic deep fryer for doughnuts, and no matter how fancy the name of the recipe you're preparing, all these confections are easily mixed and made from simple batters. There are three equally important things to control in producing them: the consistency of your batter, the surface of your griddle or pan, and the evenness of its heat. Follow the instructions on the following pages carefully to get the best results.

Dutch Baby, 56

Making Pancakes

Basic pancake batter is extremely simple—it contains nothing more than flour, leavening, and sugar (the dry ingredients) and milk, eggs, and melted butter (the wet ingredients)—and easy to mix.

To start, mix the dry ingredients in a bowl, stirring them together with a whisk to ensure that everything is well blended. There is rarely a need to sift dry ingredients, although you should always make sure that baking powder and baking soda are free of lumps—if you find lumps, pinch them between your fingers. You can mix the dry ingredients in advance and store in a sealable plastic bag or an airtight container for up to 2 weeks in a cool cupboard or 1 month in the freezer.

The wet ingredients are mixed together in another bowl. You can mix the wet ingredients together ahead of time and store covered, in the refrigerator for up to 24 hours.

When you are ready to make the pancakes, combine the dry and wet ingredients by mixing them together, preferably with a rubber spatula or a wooden spoon, using a light hand and mixing only until the ingredients are combined. It is better to have a few small lumps than to overwork the batter, activate the flour's gluten, and end up with a tough cake.

HOW TO COOK PANCAKES

To begin, lightly butter, oil, or spray your griddle, if needed, and heat over medium heat. If you are using an electric griddle, preheat it to 350°F.

1 Pancake batter should be spooned, ladled, or poured slowly and steadily from a height of 2 to 3 inches onto the griddle. To get a nice round pancake, hold the spoon, ladle, or pitcher steady so that the batter falls in the same spot. Depending on the consistency of the batter, it will either spread into a round by itself or need a little nudge with the back of a ladle or spoon or a metal spatula. It is always a good idea to make one test pancake first to check the batter's consistency and judge how much space each one will need. If, for example, a recipe produces 4-inch-round pancakes, you will need to pour the batter onto the griddle at intervals of 5 to 6 inches. Of course, if a couple of pancakes run together, it is not a tragedy, since they can be cut apart easily with the edge of a spatula.

2 Most pancakes are "bubblers." When the top of the pancake is speckled with bubbles, some bubbles have popped, and the underside of the pancake is golden brown (lift an edge with your spatula and peek at the underside to make sure), slide your spatula under the pancake and turn it, taking care not to let it fold over on itself.

3 Cook the pancake until the second side is lightly browned (lift an edge with your spatula)—it won't get as dark as the first side—which will take only about half as long as the first side did. It is best to turn pancakes just once.

Basic Pancakes

About twelve 5-inch cakes

Prepare and preheat your griddle, opposite.

Whisk together in a large bowl:

1½ cups all-purpose flour
3 tablespoons sugar
1½ teaspoons baking powder
½ teaspoon salt

Whisk together in another bowl:

1½ cups milk
3 tablespoons unsalted butter, melted
2 large eggs
½ teaspoon vanilla (optional)

Pour the wet ingredients over the dry ingredients and gently stir them together, mixing just until combined. If you wish, fold in one or more of the following:

½ cup plump raisins or other very finely diced soft dried fruit
½ cup fresh or frozen blueberries
½ cup finely chopped nuts, toasted
½ cup thinly sliced ripe bananas
½ cup crumbled cooked bacon
½ cup shredded cheese
¼ cup shredded sweetened dried coconut
¼ cup grated semisweet or milk chocolate

Spoon ⅓ cup batter onto the griddle for each pancake, nudging the batter into rounds. Cook until the top of each pancake is speckled with bubbles and some bubbles have popped open, then turn and cook until the underside is lightly browned. Serve immediately or keep warm in a 200°F oven while you finish cooking the rest. Serve with:

Pure maple syrup or honey
Pats of butter

BUTTERMILK

Buttermilk, once the residue left over from making butter, is today made by adding a bacterial culture to skim milk to produce the flavor, body, and acidity of the original product. Thus the word "buttermilk" today means cultured buttermilk.

BASIC BUTTERMILK PANCAKES

Serve these pancakes at your next brunch with seasonal fruit and pure maple syrup.
Prepare *Basic Pancakes, left,* adding ½ teaspoon baking soda to the dry ingredients and substituting buttermilk for the milk.

Cornmeal Pancakes

About sixteen 5-inch cakes

Prepare and preheat your griddle, opposite.

Whisk together in a large bowl:

1¼ cups yellow cornmeal, preferably stone ground
¾ cup all-purpose flour
1¾ teaspoons baking powder
¾ teaspoon salt

Whisk together in another bowl:

1⅔ cups milk
4 tablespoons (½ stick) unsalted butter, melted
¼ cup pure maple syrup
2 large eggs

Pour the wet ingredients over the dry ingredients and gently whisk them together, mixing just until combined. The batter will be very thin. Stir in:

¾ cup fresh or frozen corn kernels

Spoon ¼ cup batter onto the griddle for each pancake, leaving room for spreading. This is a thin, runny batter that forms irregularly shaped rounds before it sets, but the pancakes will look fine when you flip them over. Cook until the top of each pancake is speckled with bubbles and some bubbles have popped, then turn and cook until the underside is lightly browned. Serve immediately or keep warm in a 200°F oven while you finish cooking the rest. Serve with:

Pure maple syrup or honey
Yogurt

JALAPEÑO CORNMEAL PANCAKES

Jalapeños are widely available and can vary considerably in their heat from totally mild to quite hot varieties found in farmers' markets and their homeland of Veracruz, Mexico. For a spicy, savory pancake, prepare Cornmeal Pancakes, left, folding into the batter 1 fresh jalapeño pepper, seeded and minced, 2 tablespoons finely minced fresh cilantro (optional), ½ teaspoon hot red pepper sauce, ¼ teaspoon chili powder, and ground black pepper to taste.

Lemon Pancakes

About twelve 4-inch cakes

These can also be served with honey.
Prepare and preheat your griddle, 52.
Whisk together in a large bowl:

1 cup all-purpose flour
⅓ cup sugar
1½ teaspoons baking powder
½ teaspoon baking soda
¼ teaspoon salt
Whisk together in another bowl:
¾ cup sour cream
⅓ cup milk
¼ cup fresh lemon juice

3 tablespoons unsalted butter,
  melted
1 large egg
1½ teaspoons vanilla
Pour the wet ingredients over the
dry ingredients and gently whisk
them together, mixing just until
combined. Fold in:
Finely grated zest of 2 lemons
The batter will be thick and bubbly—
similar to a cake batter. Spoon ¼ cup
batter onto the griddle for each pan-

cake, nudging the batter into rounds.
Cook until the top of each pancake
is speckled with bubbles and some
bubbles have popped, then turn and
cook until the underside is lightly
browned. Serve immediately or keep
warm in a 200°F oven while you
finish cooking the rest. Serve with
(opposite):
Sweetened sour cream or Crème
  Fraîche, 87

KEEPING PANCAKES HOT

Pancakes can be kept for as long as
20 minutes before serving in a preheated 200°F oven. As the pancakes
come off the griddle, place them on
a heatproof platter, one slightly overlapping the last, and cover them very
loosely with foil. For added tenderness and moistness, brush both sides
of each pancake with melted butter
before putting it in the oven.

LEMON POPPY SEED PANCAKES

*Unless organic, citrus fruits usually
are coated with wax. If using the
zest, we urge you to use organic
fruits. Avoid citrus with deep bruises,
soft spots, or mold. In grating zest,
remove only the top colored layer, as
the white pith beneath is bitter.*
Prepare *Lemon Pancakes, above,*
folding in ½ cup poppy seeds
along with the lemon zest.

Blueberry Buttermilk Pancakes

About twelve 4½-inch cakes

Prepare and preheat your griddle, 52.
Whisk together in a large bowl:
1 cup all-purpose flour
½ cup yellow cornmeal, preferably
  stone ground
¼ cup sugar
1¼ teaspoons baking powder
¼ teaspoon baking soda
¼ teaspoon salt
Whisk together in another bowl:
1¼ cups buttermilk
4 tablespoons (½ stick) unsalted
  butter, melted

2 large egg yolks
1½ teaspoons finely grated
  lemon zest
Pour the wet ingredients over the
dry ingredients and gently whisk
them together, mixing just until
combined. Beat until the peaks are
stiff but not dry, then fold into the
batter:
2 large egg whites
Fold in:
1 cup fresh or frozen blueberries
Spoon ⅓ cup batter onto the griddle

for each pancake, nudging the batter
into rounds. Cook until the top of
each pancake is speckled with bubbles
and some bubbles have popped,
then turn and cook until the underside is lightly browned. Serve immediately or keep warm in a 200°F
oven while you finish cooking the
rest. Serve with:
Pure maple syrup, honey, or
  blueberry sauce

Silver Dollar Hots

About 40 mini pancakes

Super light and fluffy describes these delicate treats. Hot off the griddle is the best way to eat them. You can use a platar, a cast-iron pan with round indentations, for perfectly shaped cakes. Prepare and preheat your griddle, 52. Lightly beat:

2 large eggs

Whisk in:

1 cup sour cream
¼ cup all-purpose flour
1 ½ tablespoons sugar
½ teaspoon salt
¼ teaspoon baking soda

Spoon 1 tablespoon batter onto the griddle for each pancake, nudging the batter into 2½-inch rounds. Cook until the top of each pancake is speckled with bubbles and some bubbles have popped, then turn over and cook until the underside is lightly browned. Serve immediately with:

Pure maple syrup or fresh fruit

Dutch Baby

One 10-inch cake; 2 to 4 servings

Serve this straight from the oven with a dusting of powdered sugar, a spoonful of the best fruit preserves you can lay your hands on, or Buttered Apple Slices, below. Preheat the oven to 425°F. Whisk together until smooth:

½ cup milk
½ cup all-purpose flour
¼ cup sugar
2 large eggs, at room temperature

Melt in a 10-inch ovenproof skillet (cast iron is ideal) over medium heat:

4 tablespoons (½ stick) unsalted butter

Tilt the pan so that the butter coats the sides. Pour the egg mixture into the skillet and cook, without stirring, for 1 minute. Place the skillet in the oven and bake until the pancake is puffed and golden, 12 to 15 minutes. Serve immediately, for the pancake loses its puff, and therefore its drama, almost immediately.

Buttered Apple Slices

4 breakfast servings; 8 garnish servings

Melt in a large skillet over medium-low heat until foamy:

2 tablespoons butter

Add in a single layer:

2 firm, tart apples, cored and cut into ⅜-inch slices

Cook until the bottoms are golden. Turn and cook the second side until golden, a few minutes longer, depending on the firmness of the apples. Do not let them turn soft.

To glaze, especially if they are very tart, sprinkle over the surface:

2 tablespoons sugar

Let stand until the sugar melts. Serve warm.

Raised Buckwheat Blini

About fifteen 3-inch pancakes

Combine in a saucepan:

1½ cups milk

4 tablespoons (½ stick) unsalted butter

Heat until the butter is melted, then let cool to between 105° and 115°F. Sprinkle with:

2 teaspoons active dry yeast

Let stand until the yeast is dissolved, about 5 minutes. Whisk together:

⅔ cup all-purpose flour

⅔ cup buckwheat flour

2 tablespoons sugar

1 teaspoon salt

Pour the wet ingredients over the dry ingredients and gently whisk them together, mixing just until combined. Cover the bowl tightly with plastic wrap and let rise in a warm place until doubled in volume, about 1 hour. When the batter has risen, you can make the pancakes immediately or refrigerate the covered bowl for up to 24 hours. If the batter is refrigerated, let stand at room temperature for 20 minutes before proceeding.

Stir to deflate the batter and whisk in:

3 large eggs, lightly beaten

Prepare and preheat your griddle, 52.

Spoon a scant ¼ cup batter onto the griddle for each pancake, leaving room between the pancakes for spreading. Cook until the top of each blini is speckled with bubbles and some bubbles have popped, then turn and cook until the underside is lightly browned. Serve immediately or keep warm in a 200°F oven while you finish cooking the rest. Serve with:

Melted butter or smoked salmon and sour cream or *Crème Fraîche*, 87, or pure maple syrup

Making Waffles

Waffles are light, leavened cousins of the ancient Communion wafer, which, like waffles, were once baked in irons and had the same honeycomb pattern that characterizes all members of the wafer/waffle family. The earliest waffle irons were probably produced in thirteenth-century Germany or Holland. Consisting of two hinged iron plates attached to long wooden handles, the irons were designed to be held over the embers of a hearth fire. The ancient plates were far more elaborate than those of today's waffle irons, often embossed with family initials, religious symbols, coats of arms, figures, or landscape scenes.

Today, the usual pattern is simply a grid, often shallow but better, especially for Belgian waffles, when deep. Most contemporary waffle irons are square or rectangular in shape, but look for those shaped like a Five of Hearts—a circle composed of five shallow-gridded hearts—a form once popular among the Pennsylvania Dutch. Waffles were brought to America by the Dutch settlers of the 1600s, but they were probably not widely known until sometime in the next century. In the late 1700s, Thomas Jefferson traveled to France and brought back a French waffle iron at considerable trouble and expense.

A waffle batter needs butter and a fair amount of it. The butter both tenderizes a waffle and helps keep it from sticking to the iron. You can substitute oil for butter in a recipe without changing the texture—of course, this will affect the flavor—but you cannot make waffles without either butter or oil.

HOW TO BAKE WAFFLES

You can bake any waffle recipe in any waffle iron, but the amount of batter you will need for each waffle and the number of waffles the recipe yields will change. In all likelihood, in fact, you will have to make adjustments for your own iron—you may need less of a thinner batter, more of a thicker one.

1 Try a sample waffle or two to be safe. Because batters have different consistencies, some will spread across the iron's grids by themselves.

2 Others will need a little cajoling with the back of a metal spatula, wooden spoon, or ladle.

Batters should be poured or spread to within ¼ inch of the edge of the grids; when the iron is closed, the top plate will push the batter to the edge to fill the space. If you have overfilled the grids or spread the batter too far, try baking with the iron open for 30 seconds; this may stop any overflow. Once the iron is closed, do not open it until the steam has subsided. Waffles usually take 4 to 5 minutes to cook. If after that time the lid is difficult to open, do not force it, for the waffle is not yet baked.

USING A WAFFLE IRON

If you are using a stovetop cast-iron waffler, seasoning is a must. Rub the baking surfaces lightly with corn or peanut oil and wipe off any excess oil. If you have an electric waffle iron with a nonstick finish, there is probably no need to season the grids; simply follow the manufacturer's instructions. Even if seasoning is not required, the iron may smoke when it is first heated. This is normal. A properly seasoned waffle iron, with or without a nonstick coating, doesn't need to be greased every time you use it, since most waffle batters contain enough butter to keep the waffles from sticking. If you feel it is necessary to grease your iron, rub with corn or peanut oil, vegetable oil spray, or melted butter before heating the iron.

Basic Waffles

Twelve 6-inch waffles

We give you three choices to prepare this recipe: use 4 tablespoons butter for a reduced-fat waffle; 8 tablespoons for a classic light and fluffy waffle; or 16 tablespoons for the crunchiest, most delicious waffle imaginable. To toast nuts in the oven: Spread them blanched or unblanched on an ungreased baking sheet and bake in a 325°F oven for 5 to 7 minutes. Check and stir often to prevent burning.

Preheat your waffle iron.

Whisk together in a large bowl:

1¾ cups all-purpose flour
1 tablespoon baking powder
1 tablespoon sugar
½ teaspoon salt

Whisk together in another bowl:

3 large eggs, well beaten
4 to 16 tablespoons (½ to 2 sticks) unsalted butter, melted
1½ cups milk

Make a well in the center of the dry ingredients and pour in the wet ingredients. Gently whisk them together with a few swift strokes. (The batter should have a pebbled look, similar to a muffin batter.) If you wish, fold in one or more of the following:

½ cup plump raisins or other very finely diced soft dried fruit
½ cup fresh or frozen blueberries or raspberries
½ cup finely chopped nuts, toasted
½ ripe banana, thinly sliced
½ cup crumbled cooked bacon
½ cup shredded cheese
¼ cup shredded sweetened dried coconut
¼ cup grated semisweet or milk chocolate

Spoon ½ cup batter (or the amount recommended by your waffle iron's manufacturer) onto the hot iron. Spread the batter to within ¼ inch of the edge of the grids, using the back of a metal spatula, wooden spoon, or ladle. Close the lid and bake until the waffle is golden brown (see *How to Bake Waffles, opposite*). Serve immediately or keep warm while you finish cooking the rest. Serve with:

Pure maple syrup or jam
Pats of butter

or:

Hot Buttered Maple Sauce, below

BASIC BUTTERMILK WAFFLES

Prepare *Basic Waffles, above,* adding ¼ teaspoon baking soda to the dry ingredients and substituting buttermilk for the milk.

Hot Buttered Maple Sauce

About 1⅓ cups; 6 to 8 servings

When drenched with this sauce, waffles become a showpiece.

Combine in a medium, heavy saucepan:

1 cup pure maple syrup
⅓ cup sugar

Stirring constantly with a wooden spoon, bring to a boil and cook until the last drop of sauce that falls from the spoon spins a short, wispy thread. This will take about 3 minutes. Remove from the heat and add:

6 tablespoons (¾ stick) unsalted butter, cut into pieces
2 tablespoons water
⅛ teaspoon salt

Stir briskly until the butter is melted and the sauce is thick and creamy. Whisk in a bowl until light and frothy:

1 large egg

Slowly whisk the hot maple mixture into the egg. Rinse out the pan, dissolving any sugar crystals, then dry the pan thoroughly. Return the sauce to the pan and cook, stirring constantly, over medium heat until the sauce comes to a simmer and is thickened. Serve at once, or let cool then cover and refrigerate for up to 3 days. Reheat over low heat, stirring; if the sauce separates, remove from the heat and whisk in a little hot water.

KEEPING WAFFLES WARM

If you are preparing a large breakfast or brunch, you may want to bake waffles ahead of time. Waffles can be kept warm for as long as 20 minutes in a 200°F oven. Spread the waffles out in a single layer directly on the oven rack. It is important that you do not stack waffles, which makes them soggy. Because waffles freeze and reheat well, we plan for leftovers and multiply the recipe, wrapping cooled waffles airtight and storing them in the freezer. To reheat, place the still-frozen waffles directly on the rack of a preheated 350°F oven and bake until heated through, about 10 minutes.

Belgian Waffles

Twelve 6-inch waffles

When Belgian waffles were introduced to Americans at the 1964 World's Fair in New York City, they were yeast-raised and served with sweetened whipped cream. This recipe is in the spirit of the original Belgian waffle.

Whisk together:

1 envelope (2¼ teaspoons) active dry yeast

¼ cup warm (105° to 115°F) milk

Let stand until the yeast is dissolved, about 5 minutes. Whisk together in a large bowl:

3 large egg yolks

¼ cup lukewarm milk

12 tablespoons (1½ sticks) unsalted butter, melted and cooled to lukewarm

Whisk in the yeast mixture along with:

½ cup sugar

1½ teaspoons salt

2 teaspoons vanilla

Add, in 3 parts:

4 cups all-purpose flour

alternating, in 2 parts, with:

2½ cups warm (105° to 115°F) milk

Beat until soft peaks form, then fold into the batter:

3 large egg whites

Cover the bowl tightly with plastic wrap and let rise in a warm place until doubled in volume, about 1 hour. Stir to deflate the batter. Preheat your waffle iron.

Spoon ½ cup batter (or the amount recommended by your waffle iron's manufacturer) onto the hot iron. Spread the batter to within ¼ inch of the edge of the grids, using the back of a metal spatula, wooden spoon, or ladle. Close the lid and bake until the waffle is golden brown (see *How to Bake Waffles*, 60). Serve immediately or keep warm in a single layer on a rack in a 200°F oven while you finish cooking the rest. Serve with:

Pats of butter and powdered sugar or fresh fruit and whipped cream

Cornmeal Waffles

Eight 6½-inch round waffles

These can be thought of as flat, crisp corn bread.

Preheat your waffle iron.

Whisk together in a large bowl:

1 cup all-purpose flour
1 cup cornmeal, preferably stone ground
2 teaspoons baking powder
¾ teaspoon salt
½ teaspoon baking soda

Whisk together in another bowl:

2 cups buttermilk
¼ cup pure maple syrup
5 tablespoons unsalted butter, melted
2 large egg yolks, at room temperature

Pour the wet ingredients over the dry ingredients and gently whisk them together, mixing just until combined. Beat until the peaks are stiff but not dry, then fold into the batter:

2 large egg whites

Spoon a rounded ½ cup batter (or a little more than the amount recommended by your waffle iron's manufacturer) onto the hot iron. Spread the batter to within ¼ inch of the edge of the grids, using the back of a metal spatula, wooden spoon, or ladle. Close the lid and bake until the waffle is golden brown (see *How to Bake Waffles*, 60). Serve immediately or keep warm in a single layer on a rack in a 200°F oven while you finish cooking the rest. Serve with:

Pure maple syrup
Bacon

Honey Bran Waffles

Six 6½-inch round waffles

Whole-wheat flour and coarse bran, also known as miller's bran, are available at natural foods stores. Try these with slices of sharp Cheddar cheese.

Preheat your waffle iron.

Whisk together in a large bowl:

¾ cup all-purpose flour
¾ cup whole-wheat flour
½ cup coarse bran
2 teaspoons baking powder
½ teaspoon salt
¼ teaspoon baking soda

Whisk together in another bowl:

1½ cups buttermilk
⅓ cup honey
4 tablespoons (½ stick) unsalted butter, melted
2 large eggs
½ teaspoon vanilla

Pour the wet ingredients over the dry ingredients and gently whisk them together, mixing just until combined. The batter will be thick and bubbly. Spoon a rounded ½ cup batter (or a little more than the amount recommended by your waffle iron's manufacturer) onto the hot iron. Spread the batter to within ¼ inch of the edge of the grids, using the back of a metal spatula, wooden spoon, or ladle. Close the lid and bake until the waffle is golden brown (see *How to Bake Waffles*, 60). Serve immediately or keep warm in a single layer on a rack in a 200°F oven while you finish cooking the rest. Serve with:

Honey or pure maple syrup
Pats of butter

Blintzes

About twelve 7½-inch blintzes

Combine in a blender or food processor until smooth:

1 cup all-purpose flour
1 cup milk
3 large eggs
2 tablespoons unsalted butter, melted
2 teaspoons sugar
Pinch of salt

Pour the batter into a pitcher or other container with a pouring lip. Cover with plastic wrap and let stand at room temperature for 30 minutes or refrigerate for up to 2 days. Place a nonstick or seasoned crêpe pan over medium heat. Coat the pan with a little:

Unsalted butter

Stir the batter and pour 2½ to 3 tablespoons into the pan, lifting the pan off the heat and tilting and rotating it so that the batter forms an even layer. Cook until the top is dry and set and the underside is golden. Remove the blintz to a piece of wax paper. Continue cooking the rest of the blintzes, buttering the pan and stirring the batter before starting each one. Stack the finished blintzes between sheets of wax paper. Use as soon as they are cool enough to fill and roll, or let cool, wrap airtight, and freeze for up to 1 month.

Blueberry Blintzes

6 filled blintzes; 6 servings

Combine in a medium saucepan:

1 cup fresh or frozen blueberries
Juice and finely grated zest of ½ lemon
2 tablespoons sugar
½ teaspoon ground ginger
¼ teaspoon ground cinnamon

Bring to a boil over medium heat, stirring constantly, then continue to boil until most of the berries have popped and the mixture is the consistency of jam. Add:

1 cup fresh or frozen blueberries

Cook and stir for 1 minute. Transfer to a bowl and let cool to room temperature. Spoon the filling in the center of the uncooked side of:

6 Blintzes, *above*

Fold the sides of each blintz around the filling to form a rectangular package. In a large skillet, preferably nonstick, heat over medium heat:

2 tablespoons unsalted butter
1 tablespoon vegetable oil

When the butter is melted and the bubbles subside, add the blintzes, seam side down, and cook until golden brown on both sides. Transfer the blintzes to paper towels to drain for a moment. Serve immediately with (opposite):

Lemon curd or topping of your choice

Sweet Cheese Blintzes

8 filled blintzes; 4 servings

Combine in a blender or food processor until smooth:

1¼ cups (10 ounces) farmer's cheese or drained small-curd cottage cheese
2 ounces cream cheese
1 large egg
1 tablespoon sugar
1 teaspoon vanilla
¼ teaspoon salt
Grated zest of ½ orange (optional)

Transfer to a bowl and stir in:

½ cup plump raisins (optional)

Spoon the filling in the center of the uncooked side of:

8 Blintzes, *above*

Fold the sides of each blintz around the filling to form a rectangular package. (At this point, the filled blintzes can be wrapped airtight and frozen for up to 1 month.) In a large skillet, preferably nonstick, heat over medium heat:

2 tablespoons unsalted butter
1 tablespoon vegetable oil

When the butter is melted and the bubbles subside, add the blintzes, seam side down, and cook until golden brown on both sides. Transfer the blintzes to paper towels to drain for a moment. Serve immediately with:

Sour cream

Making Doughnuts and Beignets

The doughnut harks back to the Dutch *Olie-Koechen* ("fried cake"), which probably came to America with Dutch settlers of the 1640s but may have arrived even earlier, with the Pilgrims, who spent several years in exile in Holland before making their way to Plymouth.

You can fry doughnuts in any oil or solid shortening. Most important, the fat must be impeccably fresh and clean. Using a deep skillet, saucepan, or fryer—an electrtic deep fryer with a rotating basket is highly recommended—heat about 3 inches of fat to a steady temperature of 360° to 370°F, unless otherwise specified. To keep the fat at a constant temperature, fry no more than 2 or 3 doughnuts at a time, being careful not to crowd them. The easiest way to slip a doughnut into fat is to dip a metal spatula into the hot fat and then lift the doughnut with the spatula from the counter into the pan, once again immersing the spatula. It is hard to give exact cooking times. Color is a better indicator than the clock, so fry doughnuts until they are deeply golden on one side, then flip them over. When the doughnuts are done, remove them from the fryer with tongs or a long-tined fork and transfer them to a triple layer of paper towels to drain, patting off any excess fat. As soon as one doughnut comes out of the fryer, another should go in. If you like sugared doughnuts, shake them in a bag of granulated sugar while still warm or dust with powdered sugar after they cool a bit. Doughnuts taste best while they are still warm.

HOW TO MIX AND CUT DOUGHNUTS

Like cake batters, doughnut doughs are best made with room-temperature ingredients. Handle the dough minimally and chill before rolling and cutting. When at high altitudes, yeast-based doughnuts require no adjustment; for quick-leavened doughnuts, reduce the baking powder or baking soda by one-quarter but do not use less than ½ teaspoon baking soda for each cup if sour milk or sour cream is used.

1 The dough should be rolled or patted between ¼ and ½ inch thick.

2 Cut the dough with a well-floured doughnut cutter—a double cutter with a handle.

3 If that implement is unavailable, two biscuit or cookie cutters—one about 2½ to 3 inches in diameter and the other about 1 inch in diameter—will do as well.

4 Transfer the doughnuts to a piece of wax paper and let them air-dry for about 10 minutes; the slight crust they will develop will reduce the amount of fat they will absorb during frying.

Honey-Dipped Doughnuts

About twenty-four 2¾-inch doughnuts

This easy dough behaves much like a brioche dough, meaning that it will fall apart as you mix it and then come together. It is important that after adding each egg the dough be beaten until it comes together and cleans the sides of the bowl.

Stir together in a medium bowl:

1 cup warm (105° to 115°F) water
2 envelopes (2¼ teaspoons each)
   active dry yeast

Let stand until the yeast is dissolved, about 5 minutes. Add and stir until the mixture is smooth:

1 cup all-purpose flour

Cover the bowl tightly with plastic wrap and let rise in a warm place until bubbly, 30 to 60 minutes. In a large bowl, beat until creamy, about 30 seconds:

10 tablespoons (1¼ sticks)
   unsalted butter

Gradually add and beat until light and fluffy:

⅔ cup sugar

Add, one at a time, beating for about 1 minute after each addition:

3 large eggs

Add and beat until blended:

2 teaspoons vanilla
1 teaspoon salt
Grated zest of ½ lemon or ¼ orange
   (optional)

Add the yeast mixture along with:

3½ cups all-purpose flour

Mix until the flour is fully incorporated and the dough, which will be very soft and golden, wraps around the dough hook or paddle and comes away from the sides of the bowl. (If you do not have a heavy-duty mixer, the batter can be beaten by hand with a wooden spoon.) Butter a large bowl, add the dough, and turn it so that its entire surface is lightly coated with butter. Cover the bowl tightly with plastic wrap and let rise in a warm place until doubled in volume, 1½ to 2 hours. Punch the dough down, wrap tightly in plastic and then a large plastic bag, and refrigerate for at least 3 hours or overnight. (The dough will rise some and may pop out of its plastic wrap, which is the reason for the large plastic bag. You don't want the dough to be exposed to the air and develop a crust.) Working on a lightly floured surface with half of the dough at a time, pat or roll the dough out ½ inch thick. Cut with a well-floured doughnut cutter and place the doughnuts and holes on a sheet of wax paper. Repeat with the remaining half of the dough. Let rise, uncovered, in a warm place until soft and puffy to the touch, about 30 minutes.

Drop the doughnuts and holes, 2 or 3 at a time, into deep fat heated to 365°F, opposite. Fry until golden on both sides. Drain well on paper towels. Pour into a small saucepan to a depth of 2 inches:

Honey

Bring to a boil. As soon as the doughnuts are removed from the fryer and drained, poke a few holes in their sides with a toothpick. Place each doughnut in the boiling honey, count about 15 seconds, then turn it over and give the second side similar treatment. Transfer to a rack placed over a piece of wax paper. Repeat with the remaining doughnuts, replenishing the honey as needed. Serve the doughnuts when the dip has dried.

Sour Cream Cake Doughnuts

About twelve 2¾-inch doughnuts

These doughnuts have an inviting tang and a firm crumb that will recall your favorite sour cream coffeecake.

Whisk together in a medium bowl:

2 cups all-purpose flour
2½ teaspoons baking powder
½ teaspoon baking soda
½ teaspoon salt
½ teaspoon ground cinnamon

In a large bowl, beat until foamy:

2 large eggs

Gradually add and beat until thoroughly blended:

½ cup sugar

Stir in until blended:

½ cup sour cream
1 teaspoon vanilla

Add the dry ingredients and stir just until incorporated. The dough will be very soft. Pat the dough into a disk, wrap it in plastic, and refrigerate for at least 2 hours or up to 2 days. The dough will never become firm but it will be workable when cold.

Working on a lightly floured surface, pat or roll the dough out ½ inch thick. Cut with a well-floured doughnut cutter, keeping the doughnut holes too. Drop the doughnuts and holes, 2 or 3 at a time, into deep fat heated to 365°F (see page 68). Fry until golden on both sides. Drain well on paper towels and either dust with:

Powdered sugar

or shake in a bag with:

Sugar or cinnamon and sugar

Serve while still warm or within a few hours of frying.

Buttermilk Potato Doughnuts

About thirty 2¾-inch doughnuts

Potatoes passed through a ricer yield the most velvety doughnuts. Potatoes low in moisture and high in starch are described as mealy and are called bakers. *When cooked, their flesh is dry and fluffy, exactly right for baking and ricing. These are the knobby, tuber-shaped russets, or Idahos, at the market.*

Peel and cut into small cubes:

2 medium baking potatoes

Boil the potatoes in a large quantity of lightly salted water until they can be pierced easily with the point of a knife. Drain the potatoes very well, then push them through a ricer. Measure 1 cup riced potatoes; keep any leftovers for another use. Whisk together in a medium bowl:

3¾ cups all-purpose flour
2½ teaspoons baking powder
1 teaspoon salt
½ teaspoon baking soda
¼ teaspoon freshly grated or ground nutmeg

In a large bowl, beat until foamy:

2 large eggs

Gradually add and beat until thoroughly blended:

⅔ cup sugar

Stir in until blended:

1 cup buttermilk
4 tablespoons (½ stick) unsalted butter, melted
1 teaspoon vanilla

Stir in the riced potatoes. Add the dry ingredients and stir just until incorporated. The dough will be very soft. Pat the dough into a disk, wrap it in plastic, and refrigerate for at least 2 hours or up to 2 days. The dough will never become firm but it will be workable when cold.

Working on a lightly floured surface with half of the dough at a time, pat or roll the dough out ½ inch thick. Cut with a well-floured doughnut cutter and place the doughnuts and holes on a sheet of wax paper. Repeat with the remaining half of the dough. Drop the doughnuts and holes, 2 or 3 at a time, into deep fat heated to 365°F (see page 68). Fry until golden on both sides. Drain well on paper towels and either dust with:

Powdered sugar

or shake in a bag with:

Sugar

Serve while still warm or within a few hours of frying.

USING A POTATO RICER

A potato ricer is the best tool for preparing light, even-textured mashed potatoes. Look for a sturdy metal ricer with at least a 2-cup perforated bowl for holding the boiled potatoes and two long handles that, when squeezed, force the potatoes through holes in the bottom of the cup. A good ricer should come with two disks of different-sized perforations. Use the disk with smaller holes for finely riced potatoes.

Beignets

About 15 beignets

Beignets are a specialty of New Orleans, where they are traditionally served with chicory-flavored coffee.
Combine in a medium saucepan and bring to a steady boil:

½ cup water

4 tablespoons (½ stick) unsalted butter

1 tablespoon sugar

½ teaspoon salt

Add all at once:

½ cup all-purpose flour

Stir vigorously, without stopping, over medium heat until the mixture comes together and takes on a shine. Continue to cook, stirring constantly, for 2 minutes. When you remove the pan from the heat, you will notice that the flour has formed a light crust on the bottom of the pan. Transfer the mixture to a bowl. Add, one at a time, beating on medium speed for 2 to 3 minutes after each addition and scraping down the sides of the bowl:

4 large eggs

The mixture should be smooth and shiny, and should fold over on itself in a ribbon when the beater is lifted. Beat in:

2 teaspoons vanilla

Immediately drop the dough, a scant tablespoon at a time, into deep fat heated to 365°F (see page 68). Fry 4 or 5 beignets at a time until puffed and golden on both sides. Drain well on paper towels and dust with:

Powdered sugar

ABOUT
GRAINS

*T*hey say love comes when you least expect it, and that's what's been happening with grains. People pampered their whole lives with rich breakfast foods are suddenly finding that what they really crave some mornings is homely oatmeal or granola or cornmeal mush.

The quest for low-fat, high-fiber fare led to a much closer look at grains, which provide complex carbohydrates, protein, a very small amount of fat, many of the B-complex vitamins, and an essential array of minerals. By eating the six to eleven servings daily of grains recommended in federal dietary guidelines, you can consume the recommended amount of protein found in one to three small portions of meat, without the saturated fat and with much more fiber.

Good health food stores and some supermarkets will stock more than a dozen distinct grains. You'll find separate discussions of how to select the most common breakfast and brunch varieties—oats, cornmeal and grits, and rice—on the following pages, along with recipes that range from simple and healthy to downright luxurious.

Unsweetened Dried Fruit and Nut Granola, 75

Old-Fashioned Rolled Oats with Raisins and Spices

2½ cups

This recipe and the following cooked cereal are made with the old-fashioned flavors of brown sugar and spices.

Bring to a boil in a medium saucepan:

2 cups water

Stir in until blended:

1 ½ cups old-fashioned rolled oats
⅓ cup raisins
Pinch of salt

Reduce the heat and simmer, uncovered, for 10 minutes. Stir in:

1 teaspoon vanilla
½ teaspoon ground cinnamon
¼ teaspoon freshly grated or ground nutmeg

Top each serving with:

1 to 2 tablespoons light or dark brown sugar or pure maple syrup

Steel-Cut Oats with Raisins and Spices

3½ cups

Bring to a boil in a medium saucepan:

4 cups water

Stir in until blended:

1 cup steel-cut or Scotch oats or Irish oatmeal

Cook, stirring, until the mixture is thickened, about 3 minutes. Reduce the heat and simmer, uncovered, for 20 minutes, stirring the bottom of the pan often to discourage sticking. Stir in:

⅓ cup raisins
Pinch of salt
1 teaspoon vanilla
½ teaspoon ground cinnamon
¼ teaspoon freshly grated or ground nutmeg

Continue to simmer for 10 minutes. Top each serving with:

1 to 2 tablespoons light or dark brown sugar or pure maple syrup

OATS

Oats deserve attention for their nutritional value, especially for their fiber, half of which is the insoluble type that aids digestion and the other half the soluble type that lowers cholesterol.

All oats are milled to remove an inedible hull but, after that, may be either processed as groats (usually cut) or steamed and rolled to hasten cooking and prolong their shelf life. Oat groats, which we know more commonly as steel-cut or Scotch oats or Irish oatmeal, contain enough fat to warrant refrigeration; because they are less processed, they yield a chewier cereal that is less likely to turn to mush. The more oats are steamed, rolled, and cut, the faster they cook and the softer they turn. The flavor benefits of mixing oats with other grains are evident in multigrain breads and several of the cereals and granolas that follow, for the oats bring a sweetness to the mix.

Oatmeal, the all-time favorite cooked cereal, is available as old-fashioned rolled, quick cooking, steel cut, and, of course, instant.

Muesli

3 cups

Muesli, also called Swiss oatmeal, was developed in the late nineteenth century by a Swiss physician for his patients. Treat it like a dry cereal and eat it warmed or at room temperature.
Stir together in a large bowl:

1 cup old-fashioned rolled oats
1 cup boiling water

Let stand, covered, overnight. The next morning, stir in:

½ cup raisins
⅓ cup chopped walnuts or unblanched almonds
¼ cup flaked unsweetened dried coconut
¼ cup chopped dried apricots

1 teaspoon light brown sugar
Spoon into bowls. (If desired, the cereal can be warmed in a small saucepan before serving.) Pour over each serving:
Warmed milk or cream to taste

Three-Grain Apple Cinnamon Granola

6 cups

Combining two or three grains in one dish yields a sum greater than its parts in mingled fragrances and textures. Dried apples and ground cinnamon add a slightly different flavor to this mixture of oats, barley, and rye.
Preheat the oven to 300°F. In a 13 x 9-inch baking pan, combine:

2 cups old-fashioned rolled oats
1 cup rolled barley
1 cup rolled rye
Bake, stirring frequently, until toasted,

about 15 minutes. Stir in:
2 cups chopped walnuts
½ cup raw wheat germ
½ cup unsalted hulled sunflower seeds
Bake for 10 minutes. Let cool slightly, then stir in:
½ cup soy flour or dry milk powder
1 tablespoon ground cinnamon
Heat, stirring, until blended:
⅔ cup honey

½ cup vegetable oil
1½ teaspoons vanilla
Add to the dry ingredients and stir until well coated.
Bake, stirring frequently, for 10 minutes. Stir in:
1 cup chopped dried apples
½ cup raisins
Let cool. Store in a tightly sealed container. Granola will keep at room temperature for up to 5 days or for up to 1 month in the refrigerator.

Unsweetened Dried Fruit and Nut Granola

6 cups

No sugar or sweetener is added to this otherwise classic recipe for granola with dried fruits and nuts. Wheat germ contains almost as much fiber as wheat bran and more vitamins and minerals. Consider adding a teaspoon or two per serving of toasted wheat germ to any breakfast cereal. Serve the granola spooned over plain yogurt along with fresh fruit or eat it as a cold cereal.
Preheat the oven to 300°F.
Pour into a 13 x 9-inch baking pan:

½ cup vegetable oil
Heat in the oven for about 10 minutes. Stir in:
2 cups old-fashioned rolled oats
1 cup wheat flakes
1 cup rolled rye
Bake, stirring often, until toasted, about 15 minutes. Stir in:
1 cup chopped walnuts, unblanched almonds, or hazelnuts
½ cup unsalted hulled sunflower seeds

½ cup raw wheat germ
2 tablespoons sesame seeds
Bake, stirring once or twice, until toasted, about 10 minutes. Stir in:
1 cup raisins
½ cup chopped dried apricots or other dried fruit
Let cool. Store in a tightly sealed container. Granola will keep for up to 5 days at room temperature or for up to 1 month in the refrigerator.

Custard-Topped Spoon Bread

8 servings

In the oven, this quick and easy batter is transformed into moist corn bread topped with a layer of golden-crusted creamy custard. Serve it with bacon or sausage for breakfast, or even all alone—but try this luxurious dish at least once with pure maple syrup.

Position a rack in the lower third of the oven. Preheat the oven to 350°F. Place an ungreased 8 x 8-inch baking dish in the oven to heat. Whisk together thoroughly:

1 cup all-purpose flour
¾ cup cornmeal, preferably stone ground

1 teaspoon baking powder
½ teaspoon baking soda

Whisk together in a large bowl:

2 large eggs, lightly beaten
2 cups milk
2 tablespoons warm melted unsalted butter
2 tablespoons sugar
1½ tablespoons white vinegar
½ teaspoon salt

Add the dry ingredients to the wet ingredients and stir just until the batter is smooth and free of lumps. Add to the heated baking dish and tilt to coat the bottom:

2 teaspoons butter, softened or melted

Scrape the batter into the baking dish and spread evenly. Set the dish on the oven rack. Pour over the batter slowly, without stirring:

1 cup heavy cream

Bake until the custard layer on top is puffed and golden brown but still quivery and a knife inserted in the center comes out clean, 45 to 50 minutes. Remove from the oven and let stand for about 10 minutes before serving. Serve hot or warm.

Baked Cheese Grits

4 servings

Grits are a favorite dish throughout the American South, where they were eaten by Native Americans long before the colonists arrived. They can be cooked plain and served by the spoonful straight from the pot, eaten (like pasta or polenta) with any number of toppings, or enriched with butter, onions, garlic, and cheese and baked in a casserole, as they are here. We like to use Cheddar cheese, but you could use Parmesan or a combination of the two.

Bring to a boil in a large saucepan:

5 cups water

Meanwhile, melt in a small skillet over medium heat:

4 tablespoons (½ stick) butter

Add and cook, stirring, until translucent, about 5 minutes:

½ cup chopped onions

Stir in and cook for 1 minute more:

1 clove garlic, finely minced

Remove from the heat. Stir into the boiling water:

1 cup grits

1 teaspoon salt

Cover and cook, stirring occasionally, over low heat until thickened, about 20 minutes.

Preheat the oven to 350°F. Butter a 2-quart casserole or soufflé dish. Add the onion mixture to the grits along with:

2 cups grated Cheddar cheese

Whisk together until blended:

½ cup milk

2 large eggs

¼ teaspoon ground red pepper

Gradually stir into the grits. Transfer to the casserole. Bake until a toothpick inserted in the center comes out clean, 50 to 60 minutes.

SOUFFLÉED CHEESE GRITS

Prepare *Baked Cheese Grits, above,* substituting 2 large egg whites for the eggs. Beat the egg whites until soft peaks form, then fold into the grits just before spooning into the casserole. Bake as directed.

Cornmeal Mush

About 4 cups; 4 servings

Stir together in the top of a double boiler:

1 cup white or yellow cornmeal

½ cup cold water

1 teaspoon salt, or to taste

Gradually stir in:

4 cups boiling water, or 2 cups boiling water and 2 cups boiling milk

Stir until smooth. Place directly over the heat and cook, stirring, until the mixture boils, about 2 minutes. Place the top of the double boiler over boiling water. Cover and cook, stirring often, for 25 to 30 minutes. Spoon into bowls and drizzle over the top:

Melted butter

Molasses, pure maple syrup, sorghum, or honey

CORNMEAL AND GRITS

Corn on the cob previews the subtle sweetness of dried corn in all its forms. The very sweetest dried corn comes from the same ears sold as fresh, but we have not seen it sold outside Pennsylvania Dutch farm areas, where the kernels are rehydrated as stewed or creamed corn. The corn raised for drying and milling and sold as cornmeal, hominy, and grits is starchier and much less sugary; yet its flavor recalls the opulence of a cornfield ripe for harvest.

Dried corn is processed for hot breakfast cereal and side dishes in two basic ways. If it is simply ground, the product is cornmeal, and coarse, medium, or fine grind can be used in any recipe unless otherwise specified. If you buy stone-ground cornmeal, you are getting the oily germ with the starchy endosperm; the product has a higher fiber and mineral content, and it must be refrigerated. The more commonly available enriched degerminated cornmeal has lost its germ and thus has a more stable shelf life.

Made with either white or yellow cornmeal, cornmeal mush is a favorite breakfast food served with butter, molasses, sorghum, maple syrup, or honey. Buy cornmeal in amounts you can use within 1 month and store cornmeal in tightly covered jars in the pantry or refrigerate for up to 2 months.

Kedgeree

4 servings

A relative of the Indian khichri, a dish made of rice, lentils, and spices. The English, it seems, substituted smoked fish for lentils and added chopped egg.

Bring to a boil in a medium saucepan:

1 cup heavy cream

Add:

¼ teaspoon ground red pepper
¼ teaspoon turmeric

½ teaspoon salt

Simmer for 2 minutes. Add and heat through:

3 cups cooked long-grain rice, preferably basmati or jasmine

Cut on a diagonal into thin slices:

4 scallions, whites and greens separated

Fold the scallion whites into the rice mixture along with:

4 smoked trout fillets (about 8 ounces total), at room temperature, broken into 1-inch pieces

Remove the kedgeree to a 5-cup soufflé dish or casserole. Top with the scallion greens along with:

3 hard-boiled eggs, chopped

Or, butter the dish, pack with kedgeree, and unmold. Top with the scallion greens and chopped eggs.

Rice Pudding

6 servings

The all-time favorite made with medium- or long-grain rice. A kernel of long-grain rice is three to five times longer than it is wide; the cooked kernels are fluffy and separate easily. Medium-grain kernels are closer to oval in shape, less than twice as long as they are wide, and contain more amylopectin, a waxy starch molecule that makes the cooked rice denser and the kernels more apt to cohere.

Have ready a serving bowl or six 5- to 6-ounce custard cups or ramekins.
Combine in a large, heavy saucepan:

¾ cup medium- or long-grain white rice
1½ cups water
Heaping ¼ teaspoon salt

Bring to a simmer over medium-high heat, then reduce the heat to low, cover, and simmer until the water has been absorbed, about 15 minutes. Stir in:

4 cups whole milk
½ cup sugar

Cook, uncovered, over medium heat for 30 to 40 minutes, stirring frequently, especially toward the end of cooking. The pudding is done when the rice and milk have amalgamated into a thick porridge. Do not overcook, or the pudding will be solid instead of creamy once cooled. Remove from the heat, then stir in:

½ teaspoon vanilla

Turn into the bowl or cups, then press plastic wrap directly onto the surface to prevent a skin. Serve warm, at room temperature, or cold. If you wish, sprinkle with:

Ground cinnamon

The pudding can be accompanied with:

Whipped cream or a fruit sauce

Swedish Rice Pudding

8 to 10 servings

One of the greatest of all rice puddings—like a mousse, yet also creamy.
Prepare and keep hot:

Rice Pudding, above

Whisk together thoroughly:

2 large eggs
⅓ cup sugar

Gradually stir 2 cups of the hot pudding into the eggs, then stir the mixture back into the remaining pudding. Cook, stirring constantly, over the lowest possible heat just until it begins to thicken, 3 to 5 minutes. Do not allow the pudding to simmer, or the eggs will turn slightly grainy. Immediately turn the pudding into a serving bowl, then press plastic wrap directly onto the surface to prevent a skin. Refrigerate until cold. Whip until stiff peaks form:

1 cup cold heavy cream

Gently fold the whipped cream into the cold pudding. Serve at once or refrigerate for up to 2 days. Spoon into bowls or goblets. If you wish, sprinkle with:

⅓ cup chopped toasted almonds or hazelnuts

The pudding is lovely when drizzled with:

Fresh Raspberry Sauce, 92

ABOUT
FRUITS &
FRUIT SAUCES

Fruits are pure pleasure—when they are ripe. Vitamins, minerals, and fibers have no more persuasive salesman than a juicy, honey-sweet peach. Eating fruit is good for everyone, of course: every fruit, like every vegetable, contains all vitamins (except B_{12}, which is found in any dairy product), minerals, and phytochemicals—those nutrients whose health-promoting properties are forever being newly discovered.

As always, the best advice is to eat the most fresh fruit you can, and preferably to eat fruit that is local, in season, and perfectly ripe. The recipes in this chapter demonstrate how easy it is to follow that advice by serving fruit at breakfast or brunch.

Fresh Fruit Cup, 83

Shopping for Fresh Fruits

Most of the fruits in these pages can be found at a market in some part of the country—if not the supermarket, then a farmers' market, fancy grocery, or ethnic market. As much as possible, buy fruits in their domestic season, and buy fruits for canning, freezing, and preserving at the peak of the season. Produce is most reasonable in price when plentiful, nutrition is greatest when fruits have not traveled for long, and flavor is richest when fruits reach the peak of their reproductive cycle. In the summer and early fall, farmers' markets and roadside stands offer the greatest variety and generally the most flavorful selection. When, in cold weather, it is back to the supermarket, make friends with the produce manager so that when you want to sample a fruit before buying it, he or she will readily give you a taste.

The way to shop for fruits is not to make a list at home but to wait until you get to the market and see and smell what is best. This is especially true when composing a fruit mixture.

RULES FOR FRUITS

● When possible, buy fruit grown organically. Select domestically raised fruit in its season. Fruit raised in your region is even better because nutrition is greatest when fruits have not traveled for long.

● Choose healthy-looking fruit—bright, plump, and sound. Become familiar with which fruits have been waxed or sprayed and urge the produce manager to provide unwaxed, unsprayed fruits.

● Do not wash fruit until serving time, then wash especially well any commercially raised fruits or fruits you suspect have been sprayed.

● To Ripen Fruit: Underripe fruits can be ripened most efficiently in a brown paper bag. Do not crowd the fruits in the bag. Place the bag at room temperature out of the sun. Turn the bag over every day so fruits can ripen evenly. Adding an apple or a banana will speed the process because these fruits emit a harmless gas that enhances ripening.

● After ripening, most fruits keep best when stored in a perforated plastic bag in the refrigerator crisper drawer. The exceptions—avocados, bananas, citrus fruits, pineapples, and melons—can be refrigerated, but their quality is best preserved in a dark, cool (50° to 65°F) place.

● Wherever you keep them, give fruits a quick check daily. When a piece shows any sign of spoilage—mold or softness or oozing—remove it. Spoilage is infectious and will quickly ruin surrounding fruits.

● Peeling Fruit: In general, do not peel fruit if you can avoid it. More often than not, the peel is a rich source of flavor, interesting texture, and valuable nutrients. However, in certain recipes or preparations, peeling is desirable. To peel fruits with loosely attached skin, dip them in boiling water for 20 to 60 seconds, transfer to a bowl of cold water to cool, then slip off the skin.

● To Keep Fruits from Darkening: When preparing fruits whose flesh turns brown upon exposure to air, rub surfaces with the cut edge of a citrus fruit—lemon, orange, mandarin, grapefruit, or lime. A quantity of fruit can be kept in a bowl of acidulated water—mix ½ to 1 tablespoon lemon juice or white vinegar into 1 quart water—for up to 20 minutes.

● When cooking fruit, retain nutrients by cooking quickly and using as little liquid as possible. Save cooking liquids and blend some into your breakfast fruit juice.

● Because fruits are acidic, all tools and pans should be made of nonreactive materials—stainless steel, enameled cast iron, or nonstick coated.

● Dried fruits such as raisins, currants, and dried cherries benefit by being plumped before being added to a recipe. Plump them by soaking in warmed or boiling spirits, fruit juice, or any liquid in the recipe they are to be used in for 10 to 15 minutes before use.

HOW TO SEGMENT CITRUS

The only fussy preparation of citrus is segmenting the fruit for a salad or dessert. This takes not skill but time— and it is worth it. Without its tough bitter casing, the delicate citrus pulp sparkles—chefs call these sections supremes.

1 Slice off the top and bottom of the round fruit, down to the flesh. Stand the fruit on a grooved cutting board (to catch juices) and use a serrated knife to cut off the rind in even slices. Trim away any remaining white membrane.

2 and 3 Free each segment by cutting down against the membrane on either side. Lift out the segment and remove any seeds. At this point, the segments can be sliced or chopped, if desired. Squeeze all the juice from the membranes into a bowl.

Fresh Fruit Cup

10 to 12 servings

You can be sure a mix of fresh fruits will be pleasing to guests when you base it on year-round favorites, then add bright colors and flavors from fruits of the season (good proportions are about 2 pounds foundation fruits and 1½ to 2 pounds seasonal fruits). To keep the mixture from looking like a hash, cut pieces in a variety of shapes, none smaller than bite-sized. Although the fruits should be served within a few hours, you can enjoy them for a day or two—citrus juices and honey will keep seasonal fruits from darkening.

Add the following fruits and ingredients in the order given to a large mixing bowl, stirring gently every once in a while:

2 sweet oranges, peeled, seeded, and cut into bite-sized chunks

Juice of 1 large lemon
⅓ cup mild honey, preferably orange blossom, or sugar
2 green eating apples, cored and cut into medium dice
1 large ripe pear, cored and cut into bite-sized chunks
1 large banana, thinly sliced
Add 3 or 4 seasonal fruits, about 8 ounces each. Choose from:
Kiwis, peeled, cut lengthwise in half, and sliced
Strawberries, hulled and quartered lengthwise
Whole raspberries or blueberries
Pitted sweet cherries
Melon or watermelon balls
Peaches, nectarines, apricots, or plums, pitted and sliced
Seedless red grapes, stemmed

MACÉDOINE OF FRESH FRUITS

A macédoine is a fresh fruit cup flavored with spirits. Classic spirits for fruit are wines—dry, sweet, and fortified, plain brandy, fruit brandy, and liqueurs. A splash of good-quality plain brandy adds elegance to every fruit. But if there were to be one bottle in the cupboard for fruit, our choice would be maraschino. Clear cherry-flavored maraschino liqueur is incomparable with mixed fruit. Prepare Fresh Fruit Cup, left, adding ½ cup maraschino liqueur or ⅓ cup orange liqueur with the honey or sugar. Cover and refrigerate for about 4 hours before serving.

Melon and Prosciutto

4 to 6 servings

The inspiration for combining wedges of melon and paper-thin slices of prosciutto just may have come from proximity. Some of Italy's finest cantaloupes are grown not far from where some of its finest Parma hams are cured. This is one of summer's most refreshing first courses.

Cut in half and scoop out the seeds from:

1 ripe cantaloupe or Crenshaw melon (about 3 pounds), cool but not chilled

Slice each half into 6 wedges and remove the rind. Place 2 or 3 wedges on each plate. Cut into wide strips:

8 ounces thinly sliced prosciutto or Serrano ham

Drape the ham over the slices— or wrap each piece of fruit in ham. Serve at once and pass the peppermill.

MELONS

Unless otherwise noted, summer is the peak season for dessert melons— melons that are not watermelons. If a melon has no fruity perfume at the smooth (the blossom) end, do not buy it (unless it is a casaba). There should be a slight softness at the blossom end. Choose melons that are heaviest for their size with no soft spots, mold, or cracks and no strong aroma indicating overripeness. If, when you gently shake a melon, seeds rattle, chances are the melon is too ripe.

The only melons that ripen slightly after picking are the smooth, or winter, group. "Smooth" describes the rind relative to other melons.

Honeydew (below left) and Santa Claus or Christmas melons have smooth rinds, but Canary and Crenshaw melons are slightly wrinkled, and casabas have distinct wrinkles. "Winter" indicates the melons take longer to ripen than others. They are ready in the fall. The flavor of these melons is mild and their flesh pale—light orange in Crenshaw and green to white in the rest. Smooth melons are fragrant when ripe, except for casaba. Casabas are ripe when golden yellow. The stem end may be slightly greenish.

America's cantaloupe (below center), muskmelon, nutmeg, and Persian melons are in the "netted" group. Choose those in which the netting is pro-

nounced and the fragrance is as sweet as you expect the flavor to be. The flesh should be musky and orange. "True cantaloupes" have another shape. They have a smooth, hard rind and may be lightly fluted. Their orange, green, or pink flesh is intensely sweet and perfumed. The great French Charentais melon (below right) is the most prominent in this group. A small crack close to the stem indicates full ripeness.

Stunning fruits blended from all of the above are termed "tropical melons." Galia, Ha-Ogen, Passport, French Breakfast, as well as other exotically flavored fruits are available mostly from the home garden.

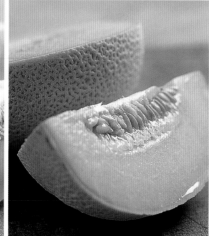

Broiled Grapefruit

4 servings

This delicious old-fashioned way with grapefruit can be served as a first course or for dessert. Pink grapefruit is preferred for its appealing color. These can be prepared many hours in advance, then sugared and broiled just before serving.

Adjust the broiler rack so the grapefruit will be about 4 inches below a gas flame or 3 inches below an electric element. Preheat the broiler. Cut horizontally in half:

2 grapefruit, preferably pink

Remove any large seeds. If desired, snip out the tough centers. Loosen each section by cutting along the membranes and skin with a small serrated knife or grapefruit knife. Place the halves on a small rimmed baking sheet. Sprinkle with:

1 tablespoon sugar

¼ teaspoon ground star anise or ground ginger (optional)

Leaving the broiler door slightly ajar, broil the grapefruit until the tops begin to brown, about 5 minutes. Remove. For garnish, quickly place in the center of each half:

1 small berry

Serve at once.

GRAPEFRUIT

White fleshed (pink) and pigmented (red) grapefruit can be found year-round. Select heavy, firm, round, or slightly flattened fruits with smooth skins. Those fruits with a brownish texture on the rind often have the best flavor. Avoid fruits with rough, puffy rinds. Marsh is the most popular white-fleshed grapefruit with few to no seeds. Star Ruby, Rio Red, and Flame are fruits of excellent quality with few to no seeds.

Apricot Compote

4 servings

When fruit is steeped in sugar, the sugar draws out its juice, forming a syrup. Here apricots are poached in their own syrup, brightened with orange. This results in a particularly rich apricot flavor. The skins toughen slightly in cooking.

If desired, peel by blanching:

10 sweet firm ripe apricots (1¼ pounds)

Cut each apricot in half along the seam line and remove the pit. Arrange cut sides up in a large shallow bowl. Spoon a little of the following into each cavity, in the order given:

¼ cup fresh orange juice
¼ cup sugar

Cover and let stand in a cool place until the sugar is dissolved, about 2 hours. Turn the fruit cut sides down with their syrup into a heavy nonstick skillet. Bring to a simmer over medium heat. Reduce the heat to low, cover, and cook until the apricots are tender when tested with a thin skewer, 7 to 8 minutes. They will continue cooking out of the pan, so do not overcook. Turn into a serving bowl cut sides up and pour the syrup over them. Cover and refrigerate for 1 hour, if desired. Serve warm or cool, sprinkled with (opposite, front):

Chopped pistachios or slivered almonds, toasted

Rhubarb Compote

3 servings

Botanically a vegetable, rhubarb has stalks that look like cherry-red celery but are less watery. Their flavor is tartness itself with a fruity aftertaste. Field-grown rhubarb is available principally in April and May; hothouse rhubarb is available in some parts of the country year-round.

Combine in a medium, heavy saucepan:

4 cups ½-inch pieces rhubarb
¼ to ½ cup sugar

Let stand at room temperature until the rhubarb exudes some juice, at least 15 minutes. Bring the mixture to a boil over medium-high heat, stirring constantly. Reduce the heat to low, cover, and simmer, stirring occasionally, until the rhubarb is tender and the liquid thickened, 10 to 12 minutes. Remove from the heat and let cool without stirring. Refrigerate for at least 2 hours or for up to 2 days. The compote (opposite, rear) will thicken when chilled.

Prune Compote

6 servings

To stew plain prunes, omit the tea and orange juice. Cooked prunes will keep for at least 2 weeks in the refrigerator.

Combine with just enough water to cover in a medium, heavy saucepan:

1 pound pitted prunes

Bring to a simmer. Reduce the heat to low, cover, and cook for 20 minutes. Gently stir in:

½ cup sugar
½ cup fresh orange juice

Add:

2 bags Earl Grey tea

Cover and cook until all the prunes are tender, about 10 minutes more. Remove from the heat and refresh the flavor by blending in another:

½ cup fresh orange juice

Discard the tea bags and remove the fruit and syrup to a container. Cover tightly and refrigerate for at least 3 hours before serving—the compote will be best the next day. Accompany with:

Cream, Crème Fraîche, right, sour cream, or yogurt

Crème Fraîche

French crème fraîche results from a specific method of cream production that thickens the cream and gives it its characteristic nutty flavor. This crème fraîche is a delicious facsimile of the real thing. You can flavor it with vanilla and sweeten it lightly to taste, whip it, and, generally, substitute it for heavy cream. If possible, avoid ultra-pasteurized or sterilized cream.

Combine in a small saucepan and heat to 110°F.

1 cup heavy cream
1 tablespoon buttermilk

Pour into a jar and keep in a warm place, loosely covered, until the cream is thickened and has a pleasant mildly sour flavor. This may take as little as 6 to 8 hours or as long as 3 days. Do not allow it to stand so long that the flavor becomes acidic or ammonia-like. (If you multiply the recipe, the culturing time may be longer.) Cover and refrigerate. The cream will thicken further when chilled. Crème fraîche keeps, refrigerated, for up to 3 weeks.

Baked Quinces

4 servings

Quinces can be difficult to core, but the results are worth it. The flesh may darken while you are preparing them, but the orange and apple juices will refresh their color. These will keep in the refrigerator for several days. Serve with Ice Cream Mixed with Whipped Cream, right.

Preheat the oven to 300°F.

Thinly slice crosswise, then cut the slices in half:

1 large orange

Scrub off any fuzz and peel:

4 medium, ripe fragrant quinces (about 1½ pounds)

Halve and then quarter, using a large, heavy knife and slowly pushing the blade down through the fruit. Cut out the cores with a small serrated knife, catching all the gritty parts (save the trimmings for jelly). Arrange a layer of quinces cut sides up in a deep 2-quart baking dish. Sprinkle with:

1 tablespoon sugar

Add a layer of orange slices. Continue layering to the top, finishing with orange slices. Add:

1 cup apple juice

Cover and bake until the quinces test tender when pierced with a thin skewer, 1½ to 3 hours. Remove from the oven and baste the top pieces with the juices. If the quinces are dry, cover them with more:

Apple juice (about 1 cup)

Serve warm or chilled with the juices in the dish.

Ice Cream Mixed with Whipped Cream

6 servings

Whip until soft peaks form:

½ cup cold heavy cream

Cover and refrigerate for up to 2 hours.

Before serving, let stand at room temperature for 10 minutes:

1 pint vanilla ice cream

Mash the ice cream in a bowl and let stand until soft and fluffy but not soupy.

Fold the ice cream and whipped cream together until blended. Serve at once.

QUINCES

To fill a room with sweet, rich fragrance, place a ripe gold quince in the middle of it. A member of the rose family, a quince looks like a pear that grew fat and lumpy with a stubby neck. Probably because they are too astringent to eat raw, quinces have fallen out of favor. But when slices are cooked until translucent and a deep shade of red, their flavor is reminiscent of rose and apple, with a touch of pineapple in the variety called Pineapple quince. Not every variety of quince reddens when cooked; some turn gold. Quinces are available in October and November. They keep for up to 2 weeks in a perforated plastic bag in the refrigerator. Handle gently, for, surprisingly, these fruits bruise easily.

Roasted Nectarines with Raspberry Vinegar Glaze

4 servings

When baked at high heat, their skins turn russet.

Preheat the oven to 425°F.

With the tip of a knife, slash on 4 sides to prevent the skin from bursting:

4 firm ripe nectarines

Place in a 9-inch baking dish or pie pan and set the dish on a baking sheet. Combine in a saucepan:

1 cup raspberry vinegar

1 cup packed light brown sugar

2 tablespoons butter

Heat, stirring, over low heat until the sugar is dissolved and the butter melted. Pour over the nectarines.

Bake for 10 minutes and baste using a bulb baster. Bake for another 10 minutes, then turn the nectarines over with tongs. Bake until they test tender when pierced with a thin skewer, about 5 minutes more. Do not overcook. Carefully pour the glaze into a wide, heavy saucepan and boil it down until thickened, about 10 minutes. Loosely cover the nectarines with aluminum foil to keep warm. Stir into the glaze:

¼ teaspoon ground black pepper, or to taste

Pour over the nectarines in a serving dish and serve.

NECTARINES

Nectarines are peaches in plum clothing. They are a stone fruit. Look for nectarines in your local market in July and August. They do not have legendary varieties, and, even at their best, they are not as juicy as peaches, but their flavors can be sublime. If you substitute nectarines in a recipe for peaches, add a small amount of orange or pineapple juice to fill in for the missing juice. Nectarines are delicious, but they are impossible to halve and pit neatly.

ABOUT **COBBLERS,** CRISPS & GALETTES

*W*ho says you can't eat dessert in the morning? As the recipes in this chapter show, some of the most homey of desserts are perfectly suited to serve for breakfast or brunch.

We love the names Americans have given their fruit-and-dough desserts over the years—pandowdy, cobbler, crisp, brown betty, crunch, slump, grunt, buckle. These desserts seem descended from puddings on one side and pies on the other. They may be based on biscuit dough, pie dough, dumplings, breadcrumbs, a crumbled flour-based topping, or cake; the fruit may be cooked under, over, or inside the dough or between dough layers. However they are made, these are plain, uncomplicated desserts—almost folklore, passed down from one generation to the next—made with whatever ingredients are available.

All these desserts are best freshly made or the morning after. Reheat them in the oven if needed, as the microwave steams and destroys a crisp topping. Serve them at the end of a gala brunch, or enjoy as a simple morning meal in itself with a cup of freshly brewed coffee or tea.

From front to back: *Half-Covered Peach Galette, 100; Half-Covered Berry Galette, 100*

Strawberry Rhubarb Cobbler

6 to 8 servings

An egg wash gives this cobbler topping a shiny, golden glaze when baked.
Position a rack in the lower third of the oven. Preheat the oven to 375°F. Have ready an unbuttered enameled cast-iron, earthenware, or glass baking pan of about 2-quart capacity and 2 inches deep, such as an 8 x 8-inch or 11 x 7-inch pan; a 12-inch oval gratin; or a 9 x 2-inch or 10 x 2-inch glass pie pan. Without peeling, cut into 1-inch lengths:

1¼ pounds rhubarb stalks
Place in a large bowl (you should have about 4 cups). Wash and pat dry:

1 pint strawberries
Hull and halve the berries; quarter if very large. Add them to the rhubarb. Stir together, then toss with the fruit:

½ cup sugar

1 tablespoon cornstarch or 2 tablespoons all-purpose flour
Spread evenly in the baking dish.

Prepare:
Cornmeal Cobbler Biscuit Dough, opposite
Roll, pat out, shape into balls, or cut into desired shapes, as described. Brush with the glaze of your choice and sprinkle with:

Sugar
Arrange the dough over the fruit. Bake until the top is golden brown and the juices are bubbling, 45 to 50 minutes. Let cool for 15 minutes before serving. Serve with:

Softly whipped cream

Peach Raspberry Cobbler

6 to 8 servings

This cobbler has a cakelike batter that is spooned over the fruit. Buttermilk makes a flavorful and tender dough with less fat than usual. Baking soda (instead of baking powder) works with the acidic buttermilk to give the batter lift. You may peel the peaches if you like, but the skins add a lovely color to the juices.

Position a rack in the lower third of the oven. Preheat the oven to 350°F. Have ready an unbuttered enameled cast-iron, earthenware, or glass baking pan of about 2-quart capacity and 2 inches deep, such as an 8 x 8-inch or 11 x 7-inch pan; a 12-inch oval gratin; or a 9 x 2-inch or 10 x 2-inch glass pie pan. Wash and wipe dry:

6 medium, ripe peaches (1½ to 1¾ pounds)

Cut in half and remove the pits. Cut each half into 5 wedges and spread evenly in the baking dish. Cover with:

2 cups fresh or frozen raspberries

Sprinkle evenly over the top and set aside:

¼ cup sugar

Whisk together thoroughly:

1 cup all-purpose flour
1 teaspoon baking soda
¼ teaspoon salt

In a separate bowl, beat until light and fluffy:

4 tablespoons (½ stick) unsalted butter, softened
⅓ cup sugar

Beat in:

1 large egg

Add half of the dry ingredients and beat on low speed just until incorporated. Beat in:

¼ cup buttermilk

Add the remaining dry ingredients and beat just until the batter is smooth. Drop spoonfuls of the batter on top of the fruit to cover it, leaving a ½-inch border all around the edge of the dish to leave room for expansion during cooking. Bake until the top is golden brown and the fruit is tender when pierced with a skewer, 40 to 45 minutes. Let cool for 15 minutes before serving. Serve with:

Softly whipped cream

Cornmeal Cobbler Biscuit Dough

1 cobbler topping

This recipe makes the perfect amount of dough for one cobbler recipe and may be varied with other ingredients, such as sour cream. While heavy cream makes the richest cobbler biscuit dough, milk is a fine substitute.

Have ready an unbuttered enameled cast-iron, earthenware, or glass baking pan of about 2-quart capacity and 2 inches deep, such as an 8 x 8-inch or 11 x 7-inch pan; a 12-inch oval gratin; or a 9 x 2-inch or 10 x 2-inch glass pie pan. Whisk together in a bowl:

1 cup all-purpose flour
⅓ cup cornmeal
2 tablespoons sugar
1½ teaspoons baking powder
½ teaspoon salt

Add:

5 tablespoons cold unsalted butter, cut into small pieces

Toss with the dry ingredients. Using a pastry blender or 2 knives, cut the butter into the dry ingredients until the mixture resembles coarse crumbs. Add:

⅔ cup heavy cream or ½ cup milk

Mix with a wooden spoon, rubber spatula, or fork only until the dough comes together and can be rolled or patted. Gently knead the dough in the bowl 5 to 10 times if needed, turning and pressing any loose pieces into the dough. Dust the top and bottom of the dough with a little flour, then roll or pat the dough with your hands to the shape of the top of the baking dish, between ¼ and ½ inch thick. Cut the dough into circles, squares, rectangles, or pie wedges, into 1-inch strips for a lattice, or trim the edges and leave it whole. You may also gently roll small pieces of the dough into balls, flatten each one slightly, and place on the fruit. If making a lattice, arrange the strips in opposite directions, weaving them if you like. If leaving the dough whole, cut 3 small holes for steam vents. Place the biscuit dough on the fruit. Lightly brush the top with:

1 to 2 tablespoons melted butter, cream, milk, or lightly beaten egg

Sprinkle with:

About 1 tablespoon sugar

Bake the cobbler as directed in each recipe, typically 45 to 50 minutes.

Mango Pear Crisp

6 to 8 servings

Mango adds perfume and subtle background flavor to the pears, and crystallized ginger in the topping piques the taste buds with a little exotic heat. Bosc or Bartlett pears are the best choice for this dessert (opposite).

Position a rack in the lower third of the oven. Preheat the oven to 375°F. Have ready an unbuttered 2-quart earthenware or glass baking dish, 2 inches deep.
Peel and core:

**6 medium, firm ripe pears (about
   2 pounds)**

Slice the pears in half and then each half into 4 wedges. Place in the baking dish. Peel and cut into ½-inch slices:

**2 slightly firm ripe mangoes
   (about 1¼ pounds)**

Toss with the pears. Stir together:

¾ cup all-purpose flour

½ cup sugar
½ teaspoon salt
Add:

**8 tablespoons (1 stick) cold unsalted
   butter, cut into small pieces**

Using a pastry blender or 2 knives, cut the butter into the dry ingredients until the mixture resembles coarse crumbs. Or do this with a mixer or in a food processor, taking care not to blend the butter too thoroughly. Stir in:

**¼ cup diced crystallized ginger
   (about 1½ ounces)**

Scatter the topping evenly over the fruit. Tap the dish on the counter once or twice to settle in the crumbs. Bake until the topping is golden brown, the juices are bubbling, and the fruit is tender when pierced with a skewer, about 45 to 50 minutes. Serve warm.

PREPARING MANGOES

To cut up mangoes, cut the flesh from the long, broad, thin-edged pit. Score the skin lengthwise in quarters and pull off the peel. For an oval mango, hold it on one thin edge on a grooved cutting board. This will help catch the juice of the mango. With a sharp serrated knife, slice down either side of the pit, which is about ½ inch thick, removing two thick pieces. Cut the remaining flesh from the pit. Cut the flesh as desired. For a round mango, peel the same way. Then, working on one side at a time, cut the fruit down to the pit in slices or cubes, carefully slide the knife down underneath, and cut the pieces free of the pit. Repeat on the other side.

Raspberry Plum Crisp

6 to 8 servings

Frozen berries work well for this dessert, as long as they are not defrosted before baking. (Thawed berries cook too quickly and will turn to mush before the plums are sufficiently tender.) If you use frozen berries, increase the cooking time 5 minutes.

Position a rack in the lower third of the oven. Preheat the oven to 375°F. Have ready an unbuttered 2-quart earthenware or glass baking dish, 2 inches deep.
Wash in cold water and dry:

**8 to 10 medium to large ripe
   plums (about 2½ pounds)**

Cut in half and remove the pits. Cut the halves into 4 wedges and place in the baking dish. Sprinkle over the plums:

**1 pint fresh raspberries, or 1½ cups
   frozen raspberries**

Stir together:

¾ cup all-purpose flour
¾ cup packed light brown sugar
½ teaspoon salt
Add:

**8 tablespoons (1 stick) cold
   unsalted butter, cut into
   ½-inch slices**

Toss with the dry ingredients. Using a pastry blender, cut the butter into the dry ingredients until the mixture resembles coarse crumbs. Or do this with a mixer or in a food processor, taking care not to blend the butter too thoroughly. Stir in:

¾ cup chopped pecans

Scatter the topping evenly over the fruit. Tap the dish on the counter once or twice to settle in the crumbs. Bake until the topping is golden brown, the juices are bubbling, and the plums are tender when pierced with a skewer, 45 to 50 minutes. Serve warm.

Apple Galette

8 servings

A galette consists of a flat crust of pastry or bread dough covered with sugar, pastry cream, or a thin layer of fruit.

Prepare:

Deluxe Butter Flaky Pastry Dough, opposite

Position a rack in the lower third of the oven. Preheat the oven to 425°F. On a sheet of parchment paper or aluminum foil, roll the dough into an 11- to 12-inch round. Pick up the edges of the paper and transfer with the dough to a baking sheet. Melt and cool to lukewarm:

3 tablespoons unsalted butter

Brush a thin coat of butter over the pastry, reserving the rest. Sprinkle the pastry with:

1 tablespoon sugar

Peel, core, and slice ⅛ inch thick:

2 large firm apples, such as Golden Delicious

Leaving bare a 1-inch border at the edge, arrange the apple slices in slightly overlapping concentric rings on the pastry. Fold the border of dough over the edge of the apples. Brush or drizzle all but about 2 teaspoons of the remaining melted butter over the apples. Combine, then sprinkle over the apples:

3 tablespoons sugar

⅛ teaspoon ground cinnamon

Bake until the pastry begins to color, 15 to 20 minutes. Reduce the oven temperature to 350°F and bake until the pastry is golden brown and sounds crisp when poked with a skewer, 20 to 30 minutes more. Set the pan on a rack, brush the apples with the remaining butter, and let cool. Serve warm or at room temperature. The galette is best served the day it is made.

Half-Covered Berry or Peach Galette

8 servings

Prepare:

Deluxe Butter Flaky Pastry Dough, opposite

Position a rack in the lower third of the oven. Preheat the oven to 400°F. On a well-floured work surface, roll the dough into a 13-inch round. Carefully slide a rimless cookie sheet beneath the dough, letting the edges of the dough overhang the sides of the sheet. Leaving bare a 2- to 3-inch border at the edge, arrange in the center:

1½ cups blueberries, raspberries, or thinly sliced peeled peaches

Scatter evenly over the fruit:

2 tablespoons sugar

1 tablespoon cold unsalted butter, cut into small pieces

Fold the border of dough over the fruit, forming a pleated half cover, with the fruit exposed in the center. Lightly brush the dough with:

Milk

Sprinkle with:

1 to 2 teaspoons sugar

Bake the galette until golden brown, 25 to 35 minutes. Let cool on a rack. Serve warm or at room temperature. The galette is best served the day it is made.

Deluxe Butter Flaky Pastry Dough (Pâte Brisée)

One 9-inch pie crust or one 11- to 13-inch galette crust

Well-made flaky pastry is a paradox—firm and crisp, but tender, light, and flaky. It derives its strength from gluten, a tough, web-like molecule that forms when flour is moistened with water and then handled during the mixing and rolling of the dough. For tenderness, pie pastry depends on fat. This dough is rich in fat and is thus soft and difficult to handle, but it yields a marvelously tender, flaky crust with a superb butter flavor. While it is possible to make this dough with butter only, a small amount of shortening makes it flakier without interfering with the buttery taste. Since this dough tends to puff out of shape during baking, you should not use it to make a crust with a tightly fluted or braided edge.

Using a rubber spatula, thoroughly mix in a large bowl:

1¼ cups all-purpose flour

½ teaspoon white sugar, or
    1½ teaspoons powdered sugar
½ teaspoon salt

Working quickly to prevent softening, cut into ¼-inch pieces:

¼ pound (1 stick) cold unsalted butter

Add the butter to the dry ingredients. Using a pastry blender or 2 knives, chop the butter into pea-sized pieces. Add:

2 tablespoons solid vegetable shortening

With a few quick swipes of the pastry blender, cut the shortening into large chunks and distribute throughout the bowl. Continue to chop with the pastry blender until the mixture resembles coarse crumbs with some pea-sized pieces. Do not let the mixture soften and begin to clump; it must remain dry and powdery. Drizzle over the flour and fat mixture:

3 tablespoons ice water

Cut with the blade side of the rubber spatula until the mixture looks evenly moistened and begins to form small balls. Press down on the dough with the flat side of the spatula. If the balls of dough stick together, you have added enough water; if they do not, drizzle over the top:

1 tablespoon ice water

Cut in the water, then press with your hands until the dough coheres. The dough should look rough, not smooth. Press the dough into a round flat disk, and wrap tightly in plastic. Refrigerate for at least 30 minutes, preferably for several hours, or for up to 2 days before rolling. The dough can also be wrapped airtight and frozen for up to 6 months; thaw completely before rolling.

HOW TO ROLL OUT PASTRY DOUGH

Flour the work surface—lightly if you are an experienced pastry maker but a bit more generously if you are starting out. Excessive flouring toughens dough, but sticking is a disaster.

1 Place the dough in the center of the floured surface and flour the dough as well. Exerting even pressure on the pin, roll the dough from the center out in all directions, stopping just short of the edge.

2 In order to keep the dough in a circular shape, each stroke should be made in the opposite direction from the one that preceded it. You can do this by rotating the dough itself rather than moving the pin. Be sure to check the dough for sticking by periodically sliding your hand beneath it; strew a little flour on the work surface as necessary. Seal cracks and splits by pushing the dough together with your fingers. If the split reopens, your dough is probably too dry. Dab the edges of the split with cold water, overlap the edges slightly, and press with your fingertips, sprinkling a little flour over the repaired area if it feels moist and sticky. Roll the dough roughly 3 to 4 inches wider than your pan.

ABOUT
QUICK BREADS,
MUFFINS &
COFFEECAKES

*Q*uick breads are so called because they are quickly mixed and, with the absence of yeast, need no lengthy rising time before baking. Thus gratification is never delayed. These breads encompass not only sweet and savory loaves to serve as mealtime accompaniments or teatime temptations in lieu of yeasted breads, but also corn breads with savory fillings, sweet morning coffeecakes, muffins, tender biscuits, and fanciful flavored scones.

So very easy to make, these delightful breads are literally a busy person's "rabbit from a hat." Homemade hot biscuits can transform the simplest meal, fresh muffins will turn a cup of coffee into breakfast good enough for a guest, and a homemade scone at four o'clock will attract the envy of workmates. For more elaborate occasions, any home cook can enhance a table with an astonishing array of quick breads in remarkably short order. It should also be noted that any coffeecake, quick bread, or corn bread recipe can be made into muffins.

Blueberry Muffins, 104

Making Quick Breads

Most quick breads are mixed in one of three ways: the muffin method, creaming method, or biscuit method. The muffin method is the simplest. First, whisk the dry ingredients. Second, whisk the wet ingredients, including brown sugar. Then combine the wet and dry ingredients by mixing or folding briefly—just enough to moisten the dry ingredients. Do not mix or beat the batter until smooth. Overmixed batters yield tough, rubbery muffins and breads with uneven shapes.

The creaming method is done with an electric mixer. All ingredients must be at room temperature. The butter is beaten with the sugar until lightened in color and texture. The eggs are beaten in, followed by the dry ingredients, alternating with the main liquid. Quick breads mixed this way are often richer and have a finer cakelike texture than other breads.

Most biscuits and scones, some quick breads, and coffeecakes are mixed by the biscuit method. The dry ingredients are mixed thoroughly; then cold butter is cut into the flour before the wet ingredients are added.

Blueberry Muffins

12 muffins

Position a rack in the center of the oven. Preheat the oven to 400°F. Grease a standard 12-muffin pan or line with paper cups.
Whisk together thoroughly in a large bowl:

2 cups all-purpose flour
1 tablespoon baking powder
½ teaspoon salt
¼ teaspoon ground nutmeg (optional)
Whisk together in another bowl:
2 large eggs

1 cup milk or cream
⅔ cup sugar or packed light brown sugar
4 to 8 tablespoons (½ to 1 stick) warm melted unsalted butter or vegetable oil
1 teaspoon vanilla
Add to the flour mixture and mix together just until the dry ingredients are moistened. Do not overmix; the batter should not be smooth. Fold in:
1½ cups fresh or frozen blueberries

Divide the batter among the muffin cups. Sprinkle with:
Cinnamon
Sugar
Bake until a toothpick inserted in 1 or 2 of the muffins comes out clean, 12 to 15 minutes. Let cool for 2 to 3 minutes before removing from the pan. If not serving hot, let cool on a rack. Serve as soon as possible, preferably within a few hours of baking.

Bran Muffins

24 muffins

Position a rack in the center of the oven. Preheat the oven to 400°F. Grease 2 standard 12-muffin pans or line with paper cups.
In a large bowl, combine and let stand for 15 minutes:
1⅔ cups wheat bran
1 cup boiling water
Whisk together thoroughly in another bowl:
1¾ cups whole-wheat flour
½ cup all-purpose flour

2½ teaspoons baking soda
½ teaspoon salt
Whisk into the bran mixture:
¾ cup honey
⅓ cup light molasses
6 tablespoons vegetable oil
¼ cup packed light brown sugar
1 teaspoon orange zest
Whisk in:
2 large eggs
Stir in:
1⅓ cups raisins

1 cup coarsely chopped walnuts
Add the flour mixture and fold just until the dry ingredients are moistened. The batter will be thick but soupy. Divide the batter among the muffin cups. Bake until a toothpick inserted in 1 or 2 of the muffins comes out clean, 15 to 18 minutes. Let cool for 2 to 3 minutes before removing from the pans. If not serving hot, let cool on a rack.

Apple Walnut Muffins

12 muffins

These are tender, flavorful muffins.
Position a rack in the center of the oven. Preheat the oven to 400°F. Grease a standard 12-muffin pan or line with paper cups.

Whisk together thoroughly:

1½ cups all-purpose flour
2 teaspoons baking powder
1½ teaspoons ground cinnamon
1 teaspoon baking soda
Scant ½ teaspoon salt

Whisk together in a large bowl:

2 large eggs
¾ cup sugar

Stir in and let stand for 10 minutes:

1½ cups packed coarsely grated or
finely chopped peeled apples
(about 2 medium), with juice

Stir in:

5 tablespoons warm melted
unsalted butter
½ cup coarsely chopped walnuts
or pecans

Add the flour mixture and fold just until the dry ingredients are moistened. Do not overmix; the batter should not be smooth. Divide the batter among the muffin cups. Bake until a toothpick inserted in 1 or 2 of the muffins comes out clean, 14 to 16 minutes. Let cool for 2 to 3 minutes before removing from the pan. If not serving hot, let cool on a rack. Serve as soon as possible, preferably the day they are baked.

MUFFIN PANS

Muffin pans should be greased or lined with paper cups. In either case, grease the top surface of the pan if you are making giant muffins with mushrooming tops. Fill the muffin cups to any level you wish. The standard is about two-thirds full. Batter for 12 standard size will make 48 miniature muffins, but only 6 to 8 jumbo. Muffin pan sizes vary, and baking times vary with them: a mini muffin will take 10 to 12 minutes, a standard-sized muffin 15 to 18 minutes, and a jumbo muffin 22 to 25 minutes.

Classic Currant Scones

8 large or 12 small scones

Serve with Clotted Cream, below. Position a rack in the center of the oven. Preheat the oven to 425°F. Have ready a large ungreased baking sheet. Whisk together thoroughly in a large bowl:

2 cups all-purpose flour
⅓ cup sugar
1 tablespoon baking powder
½ teaspoon salt

Drop in:

6 tablespoons (¾ stick) cold
  unsalted butter, cut into pieces

Cut in the butter with 2 knives or a pastry blender, tossing the pieces with the flour mixture to coat and separate them as you work, until the largest pieces are the size of peas and the rest resemble coarse crumbs. Do not allow the butter to melt or form a paste with the flour. Stir in:

½ cup dried currants or raisins

Whisk together, then add all at once:

1 large egg
½ cup heavy cream
1 teaspoon grated orange zest

Mix with a rubber spatula, wooden spoon, or fork just until the dry ingredients are moistened. Gather the dough into a ball and knead it gently against the sides and bottom of the bowl 5 to 10 times, turning and pressing any loose pieces into the dough each time until they adhere and the bowl is fairly clean. Transfer to a lightly floured surface and pat the dough into an 8-inch round about ¾ inch thick. Cut into 8 or 12 wedges and place at least ½ inch apart on the baking sheet. Brush the tops with:

2 to 3 teaspoons cream or milk

If desired, sprinkle the tops with:

Cinnamon and sugar

Bake until the tops are golden brown, 12 to 15 minutes. Let cool on a rack or serve warm.

MAKING CLOTTED CREAM

Let fresh unpasteurized cream stand for 12 hours in cold weather or 6 hours in warm weather and then put on low heat until rings form on the surface but the cream does not boil. Store in a cold place for at least 12 hours. Skim the surface.

LEMON SCONES

Prepare *Classic Currant Scones, above,* substituting for the dried currants ¼ cup chopped candied lemon peel. Increase the sugar by 1 tablespoon and use 1 tablespoon grated lemon zest in place of the orange zest.

CREAM SCONES

Heavy cream provides both the fat and the liquid in this simplest of all scone recipes.
Prepare *Classic Currant Scones, above,* omitting the butter and egg and increasing the heavy cream to 1¼ cups.

Popovers

12 medium popovers

It is important to bake popovers until they are well browned and crusty, or they will collapse.

Have all ingredients at room temperature. Position a rack in the center of the oven. Preheat the oven to 450°F. Grease a popover tin or standard 12-muffin pan.

Whisk together thoroughly in a large bowl:

1 cup all-purpose flour

½ teaspoon salt

Whisk together in another bowl:

2 large eggs

1¼ cups milk

1 tablespoon warm melted unsalted butter

Pour over the flour mixture and fold just until blended. A few small lumps may remain. Fill the cups two-thirds to three-quarters full. Fill any unfilled cups one-third full with water so that the pan does not burn. Bake for 15 minutes at 450°F, then reduce the oven temperature to 350°F and bake for 20 minutes more, until well browned and crusty. Do not open the oven to check the popovers until the last 5 minutes to avoid deflating them. Remove from the oven, unmold onto a rack, and puncture the sides with a sharp knife to let steam escape. Serve immediately or return to a turned-off oven for up to 30 minutes for extra crispness.

CHEESE POPOVERS

8 large popovers

You can bake these in eight 6-ounce ovenproof custard cups. Grease lightly and dust the cups with flour so that the batter will climb as it rises.

Have ready ½ cup grated Parmesan cheese or 2 ounces cream cheese or soft fresh goat cheese cut into 8 cubes (1 for each popover). Divide half the *Popovers, left,* batter equally among the cups, filling them about one-third full. Divide the cheese among the cups and cover with the remaining batter. Bake as directed.

Buttermilk Biscuits

Twenty 2-inch biscuits

Position a rack in the center of the oven. Preheat the oven to 450°F. Have ready a large ungreased baking sheet.

Whisk together thoroughly in a large bowl:

2 cups all-purpose flour
2 teaspoons baking powder
½ teaspoon baking soda
½ to ¾ teaspoon salt

Drop in:

5 to 6 tablespoons cold unsalted butter, cut into pieces

Cut in the butter with 2 knives or a pastry blender, tossing the pieces with the flour mixture to coat and separate them as you work. For biscuits with crunchy edges and a flaky, layered structure, continue to cut in the butter until the largest pieces are the size of peas and the rest resemble crumbs. For classic fluffy biscuits, continue to cut in the butter until the mixture resembles coarse crumbs. Do not allow the butter to melt or form a paste with the flour. Add all at once:

¾ cup buttermilk

Mix with a rubber spatula, wooden spoon, or fork just until most of the dry ingredients are moistened. With a lightly floured hand, gather the dough into a ball and knead it gently against the sides and bottom of the bowl 5 to 10 times, turning and pressing any loose pieces into the dough each time until they adhere and the bowl is fairly clean.

To shape round biscuits: Transfer the dough to a lightly floured surface. With a lightly floured rolling pin or your fingers, roll out or pat the dough ½ inch thick. Cut out 1¾- to 2-inch rounds with a drinking glass or biscuit cutter dipped in flour; push the cutter straight down into the dough and pull it out without twisting for biscuits that will rise evenly. You can reroll the scraps and cut additional biscuits (they are never as tender as the first-cut).

To shape square biscuits: Roll out the dough ½ inch thick (¼ to ⅜ inch if cooking on a griddle) into a square or rectangle. Trim a fraction of an inch from the edges of the dough with a sharp knife before cutting into 2-inch squares.

For browner tops, you can brush the biscuit tops with:

Milk or melted butter

Place the biscuits on a baking sheet at least 1 inch apart for biscuits with crusty sides or close together for biscuits that are joined and remain soft on the sides. Bake until the biscuits are golden brown on the top and a deeper golden brown on the bottom, 10 to 12 minutes. Serve hot.

Jonnycakes

Ten 3-inch pancakes; 4 servings

Jonnycakes are a form of corn pone, America's original corn bread, made with only cornmeal, water, and salt. These are extraordinary skillet corn cakes, crusty, almost crackly, on the outside, moist and creamy within, like polenta. In Rhode Island, the center of the modern jonnycake universe, jonnycakes are eaten with pure maple syrup or butter and jam.

Combine in a large bowl:

1½ cups stone-ground cornmeal
1 teaspoon salt
1 teaspoon sugar

Pour over slowly, stirring constantly to prevent lumps:

2¼ cups boiling water

Set aside for 10 minutes. Set 2 very large skillets over medium heat. (You can also use a medium-hot griddle, set to about 325°F.) Add to each skillet:

1 tablespoon butter

When the butter begins to color, dip the batter by ¼ cupfuls. The cakes should be thick (about ¾ inch) and no more than 3 inches across. Smooth the top lightly with your fingertips if necessary. Let cook at a quiet sizzle, without allowing the butter to become darker than a pale nut brown, until the underside is a very deep golden brown, 6 to 11 minutes. Cut into extremely thin pats:

1 to 1½ tablespoons unsalted butter

Lightly press 1 pat onto each jonnycake, flip with a spatula, and let cook on the other side until deep golden brown, 6 to 11 minutes more. Keep warm in a 200°F oven. Repeat with the remaining batter.

Banana Bread

8 servings

Have all ingredients at room temperature. Position a rack in the lower third of the oven. Preheat the oven to 350°F. Grease an 8½ x 4½-inch (6-cup) loaf pan.

Whisk together thoroughly:

1⅓ cups all-purpose flour
¾ teaspoon salt
½ teaspoon baking soda
¼ teaspoon baking powder

In a large bowl, beat on high speed until lightened in color and texture, 2 to 3 minutes:

5⅓ tablespoons unsalted butter
⅔ cup sugar

Beat in the flour mixture until blended and the consistency of brown sugar. Gradually beat in:

2 large eggs, lightly beaten

Fold in just until combined:

1 cup mashed very ripe bananas
½ cup coarsely chopped walnuts or pecans

Scrape the batter into the pan and spread evenly. Bake until a toothpick inserted in the center comes out clean, 50 to 60 minutes. Let cool in the pan on a rack for 5 to 10 minutes before unmolding to cool completely on the rack.

Buttermilk Crackling Corn Bread

8 servings

Preheat the oven to 425°F.

Rinse quickly, then pat dry:

4 ounces fatty salt pork

Slice off and discard the rind, then cut the pork into ¼-inch dice. Turn into a heavy 9- or 10-inch ovenproof skillet, preferably cast iron, and cook over medium heat until very brown and crisp and the fat is rendered. Remove the skillet from the heat.

Whisk together thoroughly in a large bowl:

¾ cup cornmeal
¾ cup all-purpose flour
1½ tablespoons baking powder
1 tablespoon sugar (optional)
½ teaspoon baking soda
½ teaspoon salt

Whisk until foamy in another bowl:

2 large eggs

Whisk in:

1½ cups buttermilk

Add the wet ingredients to the dry ingredients and stir just until moistened. Fold in the cracklings and all but 1 tablespoon of the fat in the skillet. Set the skillet over high heat until the fat smokes. Remove from the heat and pour in the batter all at once. Immediately set in the oven and bake until a toothpick inserted in the center comes out clean, 15 to 25 minutes. Serve at once, either plain or with:

Jam or sorghum syrup

Deluxe Sunday Morning Coffeecake

8 to 10 servings

Have all ingredients at room temperature. Position a rack in the center of the oven. Preheat the oven to 350°F. Generously grease the bottom and lightly grease the sides of a 10-inch springform pan. Sprinkle the bottom of the pan with:

Dry breadcrumbs

and turn lightly to coat. Tap out the excess crumbs.

In a large bowl, whisk together until well blended:

2 cups all-purpose flour
1 cup plus 2 tablespoons sugar
1 teaspoon salt

Add and cut in with a whisk until the mixture resembles coarse crumbs:

10 tablespoons (1¼ sticks)
  unsalted butter

Remove 1 cup of the crumbs to a separate bowl and set aside. Add to the mixture remaining in the large bowl and whisk thoroughly:

1 teaspoon baking powder
½ teaspoon baking soda

Add:

¾ cup buttermilk or full-fat or
  low-fat yogurt
1 large egg
1 teaspoon vanilla

Whisk vigorously until the batter is smooth and fluffy, 1½ to 2 minutes. Scrape the batter into the prepared pan and smooth the top.

For the streusel topping, add to the reserved crumbs and toss with a fork until blended:

¾ cup walnuts or pecans, finely
  chopped
½ cup firmly packed dark
  brown sugar
1 teaspoon ground cinnamon

Sprinkle the crumbs over the batter. Bake until a wooden skewer inserted in the center comes out clean, 50 to 65 minutes. Let cool in the pan on a rack for 5 to 10 minutes. Slide a slim knife around the cake to detach it from the pan. Remove the pan side. Let cool on the rack for 1½ hours before serving (opposite).

DELUXE RASPBERRY ALMOND COFFEECAKE

This is a moist coffeecake. A portion of the dry ingredients becomes a streusel topping, while the rest is turned into a rich cake.

Prepare *Deluxe Sunday Morning Coffeecake, left,* adding 1 teaspoon almond extract along with the vanilla. Scrape the batter into the prepared pan and smooth the top. Stir ½ cup seedless raspberry jam until smooth and fluid, then spread over the batter. For the streusel topping, omit the cinnamon and substitute ½ cup sugar for the dark brown sugar and ¾ cup ground almonds for the chopped walnuts or pecans. Add 1 large egg yolk and 1 teaspoon almond extract to the crumbs and mix with a fork, then firmly knead the mixture with your fingers until the color is uniform. Sprinkle the crumbs over the jam and bake as directed.

Sour Cream or Yogurt Coffeecake

12 to 16 servings

Have all ingredients at room temperature. Position a rack in the lower third of the oven. Preheat the oven to 350°F. Grease a 13 x 9-inch pan. Prepare and set aside:

Streusel topping, *Coffeecake Loaf with*
  ***Streusel,* 124**

Whisk together thoroughly:

2 cups all-purpose flour
1 teaspoon baking powder
1 teaspoon baking soda
½ teaspoon salt

Combine in another bowl and set aside:

1¼ cups sour cream or yogurt
1 teaspoon vanilla

In a large bowl, beat on high speed until lightened in color and texture, 3 to 4 minutes:

4 tablespoons (½ stick) unsalted
  butter
1 cup sugar

Beat in 1 at a time:

2 large eggs

Add the flour mixture in 3 parts, alternating with the sour cream mixture in 2 parts, beating on low speed or stirring until smooth and scraping the sides of the bowl as necessary. Scrape the batter into the pan and spread evenly. Sprinkle with the streusel. Bake until a toothpick inserted in the center comes out clean, 25 to 30 minutes. Let cool briefly in the pan on a rack. Serve warm.

Old-Fashioned Gingerbread

8 servings

Dark, moist, and spicy.

Have all ingredients at room temperature. Preheat the oven to 350°F. Grease and flour one 9 x 9-inch pan or line the bottom with wax or parchment paper.

Sift together:

1¾ cups all-purpose flour
1 teaspoon baking soda
1 tablespoon ground ginger
2 teaspoons ground cinnamon
¼ teaspoon ground cloves
¼ teaspoon salt

In a large bowl, beat until creamy, about 30 seconds:

8 tablespoons (1 stick) unsalted butter

Gradually add and beat on high speed until lightened in color and texture, 2 to 3 minutes:

1 large egg
½ cup packed light brown sugar

Gradually beat in:

1 cup light molasses

Add the flour mixture and stir just until combined. Stir in:

½ cup boiling water
3 tablespoons finely chopped crystallized ginger (optional)

Scrape the batter into the pan. Bake until a toothpick inserted into the center comes out clean, 35 to 40 minutes. Slide a thin knife around the cake to detach it from the pan. Invert the cake and peel off the paper liner, if using. Let cool right side up on the rack.

Applesauce Gingerbread

8 servings

This recipe contains no milk products.

Preheat the oven to 325°F. Grease and flour one 8 x 8-inch pan or line the bottom with wax or parchment paper. Bring to a boil in a medium saucepan:

1 cup applesauce

Remove from the heat and stir in:

½ cup light molasses
1 teaspoon baking soda

The mixture will foam and bubble vigorously. Let cool slightly.

Meanwhile, sift together:

1½ cups all-purpose flour
1 teaspoon ground ginger
¾ teaspoon ground cinnamon
¼ teaspoon ground cloves
¼ teaspoon salt

In a large bowl, beat on high speed until thick and pale yellow, 3 to 4 minutes:

2 large eggs
⅔ cup sugar

Gradually beat in:

⅓ cup vegetable oil

Fold in the flour mixture in 3 parts, alternating with the applesauce in 2 parts. Scrape the batter into the pan. Bake until a toothpick inserted into the center comes out clean, 40 to 45 minutes. Let cool in the pan on a rack for 10 minutes. Slide a thin knife around the cake to detach it from the pan. Invert the cake and peel off the paper liner, if using. Let cool right side up on the rack.

GINGER

Mistakenly called a root, ginger is a tropical rhizome that is thought to be native to Southeast Asia. If it is fresh and firm, it will keep for a week or so sitting on the counter. To keep longer, put it into the vegetable crisper in the refrigerator, inside a perforated plastic bag with a paper towel to absorb any moisture. Select the hardest, heaviest rhizomes. Check where the knobs have been broken: the longer the rhizome has grown before harvesting, the more fibrous it becomes, and the more fibers you will see at the break. Mature fresh ginger is hotter and to some extent more flavorful than young fresh ginger. Ground ginger, the indispensable spice for gingerbread, can be substituted for fresh, but is much hotter, so add it slowly as you taste.

Sour Cream Pound Cake Cockaigne

10 to 12 servings

A rich "plain cake" with a nuance of sour cream and a spectacular crackly brown top. Leftovers stay moist for close to a week.

Have all ingredients at room temperature. Preheat the oven to 325°F. Grease and flour one 9-inch tube pan.

Sift together:

3 cups sifted cake flour
¼ teaspoon baking soda
¼ teaspoon salt

Combine:

1 cup sour cream
2 teaspoons vanilla

In a large bowl, beat until creamy, about 30 seconds:

½ pound (2 sticks) unsalted butter

Gradually add and beat on high speed until lightened in color and texture, 3 to 5 minutes:

2 cups sugar

Beat in 1 at a time:

6 large egg yolks

Add the flour mixture in 3 parts, alternating with the sour cream mixture in 2 parts, beating on low speed or stirring with a rubber spatula until smooth and scraping the sides of the bowl as necessary. In another large bowl, beat on medium speed until soft peaks form:

6 large egg whites
¼ teaspoon cream of tartar

Gradually add, beating on high speed:

½ cup sugar

Beat until the peaks are stiff but not dry. Use a rubber spatula to fold one-quarter of the egg whites into the sour cream mixture, then fold in the remaining whites. Scrape the batter into the pan and spread evenly. Bake until a toothpick inserted into the center comes out clean, 1 hour 10 minutes to 1 hour 20 minutes. Let cool in the pan on a rack for 10 minutes. Slide a thin knife around the cake to detach it from the pan. Invert the cake, then let cool right side up on the rack.

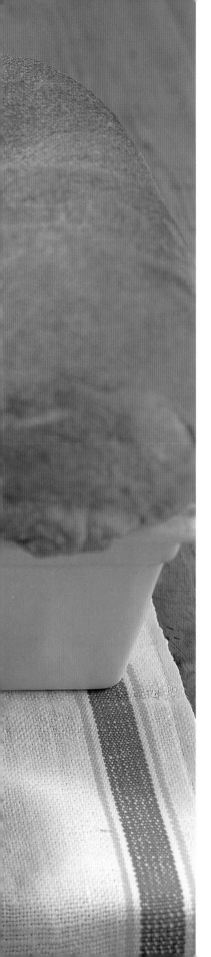

ABOUT **YEAST** BREADS

Waking up to the smell of fresh-baked bread is one of life's most elemental pleasures. As the recipes in this chapter show, it can be possible to turn out home-baked bread for a special breakfast or brunch—or at the very least to bake bread the night before and have it ready to serve the next morning.

Yeast-risen bread dates back almost four thousand years to ancient Egypt, whose bakers discovered the secret of yeast, learned how to control it, and also developed ovens for baking several loaves at a time. In medieval England, the term for "dough kneader" developed gradually into the word "lady"—an indication of the respect, we have always thought justified, with which bread bakers have long been regarded.

The tradition of baking bread in the home kitchen nearly disappeared in America in the mid-twentieth century—and commercial loaves degenerated, for the most part, into sugar-dosed presliced white bread. Many Americans grew up never having tasted a home-baked loaf. The revival of professional interest in artisanal baking in the latter part of the century has spurred home cooks to try their hand at baking once again.

Cinnamon Raisin Loaf, 117

HOW TO KNEAD BREAD

Kneading converts flour, water, and leavening into a smooth and elastic bread dough, by developing the protein called gluten. Kneading may be done in an electric mixer with a dough hook or in a food processor, but because the process is so sensual and relaxing, many bakers prefer to knead by hand.

1 All doughs should be slightly sticky when first turned out from the mixing bowl onto the lightly floured board or kneading surface.

2 When kneading by hand, grease or flour your hands to prevent sticking, then work the dough with the heels of your hands, using firm pressure and pushing it against the work surface so the dough folds over itself as you work.

3 and 4 Continue in this way, pushing the dough away from yourself, peeling it off the surface, re-forming it into a loose ball, and giving it a quarter turn (use a pastry scraper to help turn the dough if it is supposed to be soft), for about 10 minutes, until the gluten has developed.

5 When finished, most doughs should be smooth and elastic, and tacky rather than sticky. To test, slowly and gently stretch a small piece of dough, turning it in a circular motion as you pull so that it stretches evenly. The dough should hold together without tearing until it forms a sheer membrane, thin enough to let light come through.

6 Alternately, you may simply test the temperature of the dough with an instant-read thermometer; the center of the dough should register 77° to 80°F.

Cinnamon Raisin Loaf

One 8½ x 4½-inch loaf

A favorite breakfast treat. The milk, egg, and butter impart a delicate rich flavor, tender crumb, and soft golden brown crust. The dough is also easily shaped into rolls.

Combine in a large mixing bowl or in the bowl of a heavy-duty mixer and let stand until the yeast is dissolved, about 5 minutes:

1 package (2¼ teaspoons) active dry yeast
3 tablespoons warm (105° to 115°F) water

Add:

1 cup whole or low-fat milk, warmed to 105° to 115°F
5 tablespoons melted butter or margarine
3 tablespoons sugar
1 large egg
1 teaspoon salt

Mix by hand or on low speed for 1 minute. Gradually stir in:

2 cups bread flour

Gradually add until the dough is moist but not sticky:

1½ to 2 cups all-purpose flour

Knead for about 10 minutes by hand or with the dough hook on low to medium speed until the dough is smooth and elastic. Transfer the dough to an oiled bowl and turn it over once to coat with oil. Cover loosely with plastic wrap and let rise in a warm place (75° to 80°F) until doubled in volume, 1 to 1½ hours. While the dough is rising, place in a small saucepan with enough cold water to cover by ½ inch:

½ cup raisins

Bring to a boil, drain well, and let cool. Stir together:

2 tablespoons sugar
2 teaspoons ground cinnamon

Grease an 8½ x 4½-inch (6-cup) loaf pan. Punch the dough down. Using a rolling pin, roll the dough into an 8-inch-wide rectangle, about ½ inch thick. Brush the surface of the dough with:

1½ teaspoons melted butter

Sprinkle all but 2 teaspoons of the cinnamon mixture over the dough, then spread the raisins evenly over the surface. Starting from one 8-inch side, roll up the dough as you would a jelly roll. Pinch the seam and ends closed. Place seam side down in the pan. Cover loosely with oiled plastic wrap and let rise in a warm place until doubled in volume, 1 to 1½ hours.

Preheat the oven to 375°F. Whisk together and brush over the top of the loaf:

1 egg
Pinch of salt

Sprinkle the top of the dough with the remaining cinnamon mixture. Bake until the crust is deep golden brown and the bottom of the loaf sounds hollow when tapped, 40 to 45 minutes. Remove the loaf from the pan to a rack. While the bread is still hot, brush the top with:

2 teaspoons melted butter

Let cool completely before slicing.

KNEADING BY ELECTRIC MIXER OR FOOD PROCESSOR

When kneading by electric mixer, you will need a fairly powerful one with a dough hook, unless your dough is very wet. Make sure that the mixer bowl is large enough to hold the dough with room left over. Work the dough on low speed for about 3 minutes, until the dough is smooth and cleans the sides of the bowl. Continue to knead for about 7 minutes more. Knead the dough for a minute or two longer if necessary, but do not overdo it. Food processors mix and knead dough like lightning, in less than 2 minutes. Remember that caution should be taken when using a food processor not to ruin a dough by overmixing. Those with plastic dough blades can mix and knead bread dough in less than 2 minutes. Larger machines will handle 7 to 8 cups flour for 2 loaves of bread. Some smaller machines will handle 3 to 3½ cups flour for 1 loaf of bread. (Be certain to check the machine's instructions before use to determine capacity.)

Four-Strand Braided Challah

1 braided loaf

This traditional Jewish Sabbath bread is a sort of butterless brioche. It is particularly good at breakfast time.

Combine in a large mixing bowl or the bowl of a heavy-duty mixer and let stand until the yeast is dissolved, about 5 minutes:

1 package (2¼ teaspoons) active dry yeast

½ cup warm (105° to 115°F) water

Add:

½ cup all-purpose flour

2 large eggs, lightly beaten

2 egg yolks, lightly beaten

3 tablespoons vegetable oil

3 tablespoons sugar

1¼ teaspoons salt

Mix by hand or on low speed until thoroughly blended. Gradually stir in:

2½ cups bread flour

Knead for about 8 minutes by hand or with the dough hook on low to medium speed until the dough is smooth and elastic and no longer sticks to your hands or the bowl. Transfer the dough to an oiled bowl and turn it over once to coat with oil. Cover with plastic wrap and let rise in a warm place (75° to 80°F) until doubled in volume, 1 to 1½ hours. Punch the dough down, knead briefly, and refrigerate covered until it has again nearly doubled in volume (a three-quarter rise is sufficient), 4 to 12 hours. The dough is now ready to be shaped.

Weigh and divide the dough equally into 4 pieces. On an unfloured work surface, roll into balls and let rise, loosely covered with plastic wrap, for 10 minutes. Grease a baking sheet and sprinkle it with:

Cornmeal

Roll the balls of dough into long ropes about 1 inch thick and 20 inches long, slightly tapering the ends. Dust the ropes of dough with:

Rye flour

so they will be distinctly separated. Arrange the 4 ropes side by side and pinch the top ends securely together. Braid the strips of dough in the following sequence, as shown opposite: Lift and place the fourth strand over the second. Lift and place the first strand over the third, then lift and place the second over the third. Repeat this sequence, placing the strand that is now the fourth over the second, the first over the third, then the second over the third. Continue braiding until you reach the end of the strands. Pinch the bottom ends together and tuck both top and bottom ends underneath the braid. Set the loaf on the baking sheet. Whisk together and brush over the top of the loaf:

1 egg

Pinch of salt

Loosely cover the braid with lightly oiled plastic wrap and let rise in a warm place until not quite doubled, about 45 minutes.

Preheat the oven to 375°F. Brush the loaf again with egg wash. If desired, sprinkle with:

1 tablespoon poppy or sesame seeds

Bake until the crust is golden brown and the bottom of the loaf sounds hollow when tapped, 30 to 35 minutes. Let cool completely on a rack.

THREE-STRAND BRAIDED CHALLAH

Anyone who has ever braided hair or rope will have no trouble making challah braids. You can divide the dough into as many strands as you like and braid accordingly, but this one is a simple three-strand challah braid, simpler to shape, in fact, than the four-strand braided loaf above.

Prepare the dough for *Four-Strand Braided Challah, above.* Weigh and divide the dough equally into 3 pieces. On an unfloured work surface, roll into balls and let rest, loosely covered with plastic wrap, for 10 minutes. Grease a baking sheet and sprinkle it with cornmeal.

Roll each ball into a 13- to 14-inch-long rope, about 1½ inches thick and slightly tapered at the ends. Dust the 3 dough ropes with rye flour so they will be more distinctly separated. Place the 3 dough ropes side by side and pinch the top ends together. Lift the left dough rope and place it between the right and middle ropes. Lift the right rope and place it between the left and middle ropes, then the left rope between the right and middle ropes and so on until you reach the ends. Tuck both ends of the braid underneath the loaf and set it on the baking sheet. Finish as directed for *Four-Strand Braided Challah.*

Hot Cross Buns

18 buns

Place in a small saucepan with just enough water to cover by ½ inch:

½ cup dried currants or raisins

Bring the water to a boil, then drain well. Transfer the currants to a small bowl and sprinkle with:

2 tablespoons water

Cover and let soak at least 30 minutes. Stir together:

¼ teaspoon ground cinnamon

⅛ teaspoon freshly grated or ground nutmeg

⅛ teaspoon ground ginger

Prepare:

Cinnamon Raisin Loaf dough, 117

through the first rise, adding the spice mixture to the bread flour, and adding the drained currants toward the end of the kneading. Divide the dough equally into 18 pieces, about 1 ounce each. Grease a baking sheet. On an unfloured surface, roll the dough pieces into balls and place them 2 inches apart on the baking sheet. For the egg wash, whisk together:

1 egg

Pinch of salt

Brush over the tops of the rolls. Cover with oiled plastic wrap and let

rise in a warm place until doubled in volume, about 1 hour.

Preheat the oven to 425°F. Brush the rolls again with the egg wash. Bake the rolls until the crust is golden brown and the bottom sounds hollow when tapped, about 15 minutes. While the rolls are baking, make a glaze by stirring together:

½ cup powdered sugar

1 tablespoon fresh lemon juice

While the rolls are still slightly warm, decorate each one with glaze in the shape of a cross (opposite).

Crumpets

12 crumpets

Muffin rings, real or improvised, are essential for making crumpets.

Warm to 105° to 115°F:

1¼ cups water

1¼ cups milk

Pour ¼ cup of the milk mixture into a large bowl of a heavy-duty mixer. Sprinkle with:

1 package (2¼ teaspoons) active dry yeast

Let stand until the yeast is dissolved, about 5 minutes.

Add:

3 cups all-purpose flour

1 tablespoon melted butter or margarine

1 tablespoon sugar

1½ teaspoons salt

Mix by hand or on low speed while slowly pouring in the remaining milk mixture. Stir by hand for about 2 minutes or on medium speed for about 3 minutes. This is a very liquid, batterlike dough. Cover with

plastic wrap and let rise in a warm place (75° to 80°F) until doubled in volume, about 1½ hours.

Stir together until the baking soda is dissolved:

1 teaspoon baking soda

1 tablespoon water

Stir the baking soda mixture into the dough. Cover loosely with plastic wrap and let rise in a warm place for 30 minutes. Heat a cast-iron skillet or other heavy skillet or griddle and add:

1 tablespoon butter or margarine

Butter 3½- to 4-inch muffin rings (or 8-ounce pineapple cans with the tops and bottoms cleanly cut out). When the skillet is fairly hot, place the rings on the skillet and spoon a scant ½ cup batter into each ring. Cook over medium-low heat until the batter rises and becomes bubbly on top and the underside is brown. Using a metal spatula, turn both the

ring and crumpet over. Remove the ring and cook the crumpet until the underside is golden brown, about 3 minutes longer. Remove to a rack to cool. When ready to eat, heat the crumpets in the oven or toast them. Serve with:

Butter and jam or jelly

STORING BREAD

Always let bread cool completely before wrapping it for storage. All loaves can be stored in plastic wrap, though the crust will soften. Bread boxes and dry, cool, ventilated drawers or containers are also acceptable. Refrigeration tends to dry out bread, but well-wrapped loaves can be frozen for up to 3 months. Once thawed, however, they dry out more rapidly than fresh-baked bread.

Kouglof (Kugelhopf)

1 loaf

This slightly sweet decorative loaf comes from the Alsace region of France. Kouglof should be baked in a fluted ring mold. An earthenware mold is traditional, but metal or glass molds work just as well. You can also use a plain tube or Bundt pan.

Place in a small saucepan with enough cold water to cover by ½ inch:

½ cup currants

Bring the water to a boil, then drain well. Transfer the currants to a small bowl and sprinkle with:

2 tablespoons rum or water

Cover and let soak for at least 30 minutes or up to 3 days.

Combine in a large mixing bowl or the bowl of a heavy-duty mixer and let stand until the yeast is dissolved, about 5 minutes:

1 package (2¼ teaspoons) active dry yeast

½ cup whole milk, warmed to 105° to 115°F

Add:

1 cup all-purpose flour

3 large eggs, lightly beaten

¼ cup sugar

1 teaspoon salt

Mix by hand or on low speed until blended. Gradually stir in:

1¾ cups bread flour

Mix for about 3 minutes until all the ingredients are blended. Knead by hand for about 20 minutes or with the dough hook on low to medium speed for about 7 minutes.

Because this is a rather sticky dough, hand kneading requires a particular technique: Slap the dough down on the work surface, lift half of it upward with both hands (part of it will remain stuck to the table, which is normal), and slap it down over onto itself. Repeat this until the dough is smooth and elastic and no longer sticky. Add:

10 tablespoons (1¼ sticks) very soft butter

Vigorously knead in the butter until completely incorporated and the dough is once again smooth. Drain the soaked currants and knead them into the dough just enough to incorporate them. Place the dough in a buttered large bowl, cover with plastic wrap, and let rise in a warm place (75° to 80°F) until doubled in volume, about 1½ hours.

Punch the dough down, knead briefly, and refrigerate, covered, for 4 to 12 hours. If the dough has doubled, punch it down and shape it. If it has not yet doubled, let it finish rising in a warm place, then

punch it down and refrigerate for 30 minutes. Roll the dough on an unfloured work surface into a ball. Cover with plastic wrap and let rest for 10 minutes. Butter a 7- to 8-cup kouglof mold or tube or Bundt pan. Sprinkle the bottom of the mold with:

¼ cup slivered almonds

Or place in the indentations in the bottom of the mold:

Whole almonds

Lightly dust the center of the dough ball with flour. Make a small hole in the center with your fingertips and gently stretch the dough to enlarge the hole just enough so that it fits around the tube in the center of the mold. Place the dough ring in the mold, cover with plastic wrap, and let rise in a warm place until doubled in volume, about 1 hour.

Preheat the oven to 375°F. Bake the kouglof until golden brown and a knife inserted in the middle of the loaf comes out clean, about 45 minutes. Immediately unmold the kouglof onto a rack. Dust the top with:

Powdered sugar

Let cool completely. Just before serving, dust the top a second time with more:

Powdered sugar

Coffeecake Loaf with Streusel

One 9 x 5-inch loaf

Combine in a large mixing bowl or the bowl of a heavy-duty mixer and let stand until the yeast is dissolved, about 5 minutes:

1 package (2¼ teaspoons) active dry yeast

¼ cup warm (105° to 115°F) water

Add:

½ cup cake flour

⅓ cup sugar

1 teaspoon salt

2 large eggs, lightly beaten

¼ cup milk

1 teaspoon vanilla

Mix by hand or on low speed until blended. Gradually stir in:

2 cups bread flour

Mix for 1 minute until the dough comes together. Knead by hand for about 10 minutes or with the dough hook on low to medium speed for 5 to 7 minutes until the dough is smooth and elastic and no longer sticks to your hands or the bowl. Add:

6 tablespoons very soft butter

Vigorously knead in the butter until completely incorporated and the dough is once again smooth. Place the dough in a large buttered bowl. Cover with plastic wrap and let rise in a warm place (75° to 80°F) until doubled in volume, about 1½ hours. Punch down the dough, knead briefly, and refrigerate, covered, until doubled again, 4 to 12 hours. Punch down the dough and shape it. If it has not yet doubled, let the dough finish rising in a warm place, punch it down, and refrigerate for 30 minutes.

Butter a 9 x 5-inch loaf pan.

To make the streusel topping, blend with a fork or pulse in a food processor until the mixture resembles coarse crumbs:

⅔ cup all-purpose flour

⅔ cup finely chopped walnuts

⅔ cup packed light brown sugar

5 tablespoons unsalted butter, melted

1 teaspoon ground cinnamon

¼ teaspoon salt

Roll out the dough to a 12 x 9-inch rectangle, about ⅓ inch thick. Brush the surface with:

1½ teaspoons melted butter

Sprinkle evenly with half the streusel topping along with:

⅓ cup chopped walnuts (optional)

Starting from one short side, roll up the dough as you would a jelly roll. Place seam side down in the loaf pan, cover loosely with plastic wrap, and let rise in a warm place until doubled in volume, about 1½ hours. Preheat the oven to 375°F.

Whisk together and brush over the top of the loaf:

1 egg

Pinch of salt

Sprinkle the remaining streusel topping over the dough. Bake the loaf until golden brown and a knife inserted in the center comes out clean, about 45 minutes. Unmold the loaf onto a rack and let cool.

Sticky Buns

8 buns

Prepare:

Coffeecake Loaf with Streusel, above, through the first rise.

Butter a 13 x 9-inch baking pan. Bring to a boil in a small saucepan over medium heat, stirring to dissolve the sugar:

1 cup packed dark brown sugar

8 tablespoons (1 stick) butter

¼ cup honey

Remove from the heat and stir in:

¾ cup chopped pecans (optional)

Pour the hot syrup into the baking pan and spread it evenly. Let cool. Roll out the dough to a 16 x 12-inch rectangle. Brush the dough with:

1 tablespoon melted butter

Sprinkle with:

⅓ cup packed dark brown sugar

2 teaspoons ground cinnamon

Starting from one long side, roll up the dough as you would a jelly roll. Cut crosswise into 8 slices. Arrange the slices cut side down in the prepared pan, spacing the slices equally in the pan. Cover the pan with plastic wrap and let rise at room temperature until doubled in volume, about 1 hour.

Preheat the oven to 350°F.

Bake until the buns are golden brown and the syrup is bubbling hot, about 30 minutes. Let the buns cool in the pan for 5 minutes, then invert the pan onto a baking sheet to collect the hot syrup. Serve warm or at room temperature, pulling the sticky buns (opposite) apart at the seams.

ACKNOWLEDGMENTS

Special thanks to my wife and editor in residence, Susan; our indispensable assistant and comrade, Mary Gilbert; and our friends and agents, Gene Winick and Sam Pinkus. Much appreciation also goes to Simon & Schuster, Scribner, and Weldon Owen for their devotion to this project. Thank you Carolyn, Susan, Bill, Marah, John, Terry, Roger, Gaye, Val, Norman, and all the other capable and talented folks who gave a part of themselves to the Joy of Cooking All About series.

My eternal appreciation goes to the food experts, writers, and editors whose contributions and collaborations are at the heart of Joy—especially Stephen Schmidt. He was to the 1997 edition what Chef Pierre Adrian was to Mom's final editions of Joy. Thank you one and all.

Ethan Becker

FOOD EXPERTS, WRITERS, AND EDITORS
Selma Abrams, Jody Adams, Samia Ahad, Bruce Aidells, Katherine Alford, Deirdre Allen, Pam Anderson, Elizabeth Andoh, Phillip Andres, Alice Arndt, John Ash, Nancy Baggett, Rick and Deann Bayless, Lee E. Benning, Rose Levy Beranbaum, Brigit Legere Binns, Jack Bishop, Carole Bloom, Arthur Boehm, Ed Brown, JeanMarie Brownson, Larry Catanzaro, Val Cipollone, Polly Clingerman, Elaine Corn, Bruce Cost, Amy Cotler, Brian Crawley, Gail Damerow, Linda Dann, Deirdre Davis, Jane Spencer Davis, Erica De Mane, Susan Derecskey, Abigail Johnson Dodge, Jim Dodge, Aurora Esther, Michele Fagerroos, Eva Forson, Margaret Fox, Betty Fussell, Mary Gilbert, Darra Goldstein, Elaine Gonzalez, Dorie Greenspan, Maria Guarnaschelli, Helen Gustafson, Pat Haley, Gordon Hamersley, Melissa Hamilton, Jessica Harris, Hallie Harron, Nao Hauser, William Hay, Larry Hayden, Kate Hays, Marcella Hazan, Tim Healea, Janie Hibler, Lee Hofstetter, Paula Hogan, Rosemary Howe, Mike Hughes, Jennifer Humphries, Dana Jacobi, Stephen Johnson, Lynne Rossetto Kasper, Denis Kelly, Fran Kennedy, Johanne Killeen and George Germon, Shirley King, Maya Klein, Diane M. Kochilas, Phyllis Kohn, Aglaia Kremezi, Mildred Kroll, Loni Kuhn, Corby Kummer, Virginia Lawrence, Jill Leigh, Karen Levin, Lori Longbotham, Susan Hermann Loomis, Emily Luchetti, Stephanie Lyness, Karen MacNeil, Deborah Madison, Linda Marino, Kathleen McAndrews, Alice Medrich, Anne Mendelson, Lisa Montenegro, Cindy Mushet, Marion Nestle, Toby Oksman, Joyce O'Neill, Suzen O'Rourke, Russ Parsons, Holly Pearson, James Peterson, Marina Petrakos, Mary Placek, Maricel Presilla, Marion K. Pruitt, Adam Rapoport, Mardee Haidin Regan, Peter Reinhart, Sarah Anne Reynolds, Madge Rosenberg, Nicole Routhier, Jon Rowley, Nancy Ross Ryan, Chris Schlesinger, Stephen Schmidt, Lisa Schumacher, Marie Simmons, Nina Simonds, A. Cort Sinnes, Sue Spitler, Marah Stets, Molly Stevens, Christopher Stoye, Susan Stuck, Sylvia Thompson, Jean and Pierre Troisgros, Jill Van Cleave, Patricia Wells, Laurie Wenk, Caroline Wheaton, Jasper White, Jonathan White, Marilyn Wilkenson, Carla Williams, Virginia Willis, John Willoughby, Deborah Winson, Lisa Yockelson.

Weldon Owen wishes to thank the following people for their generous assistance and support in producing this book: Desne Border, Ken DellaPenta, and Joan Olson.